The Human Computer

The Human Computer

What Automation Teaches Us About Surviving AI

From an Engineer Building the Systems Everyone Fears

Ivan Daunis

The Human Computer: What Automation Teaches Us About Surviving AI

Published by Slavinsky

ISBN: 979-8-218-90249-0 (paperback)

First Edition: 2025

Disclaimer: The information in this book is based on the author's personal experience and opinions. While the author has made every effort to ensure accuracy, this book is not intended as professional career, legal, or financial advice. Readers should consult appropriate professionals for specific guidance.

Cover design by Sonia G Garcia

linkedin.com/in/ivan-daunis

For Sonia, my partner in all things,
and Alice, my greatest teacher

Preface

This book is about reinventing yourself—a process that requires continuous learning throughout life.

Learning is intrinsic to the human experience. We are designed to never stop learning. Our brains remain healthy and vital as long as they create new neural connections, growing smarter with age rather than declining.[1] When we stop learning, it's not due to biological limitations but to misconceptions about aging embedded in our social and economic structures.

I've spent more than 30 years in software development, and every 2-3 years I've experienced the effects of disruptive technology that completely transformed the industry: the Internet, the Web, Open Source, Mobile, Social Networks, SaaS, Web 2.0, Video Streaming, Cloud Computing, APIs, Virtualization, Big Data, Kubernetes, Machine Learning, Blockchain, VR/AR, Generative AI, Agentic AI—and the list will continue.

With each disruption, some jobs disappeared while many new ones emerged. Every single time, there was an opportunity to reinvent myself. I took it. Every time. Not because I'm special, but because I recognized the pattern.

Many jobs will become extinct, but many others will be created. The question isn't whether change is coming or what will be left of us—it's whether we'll embrace the opportunity to learn and adapt, and what we WANT to do when freed from work we only did because it was

---

[1] Doidge, "The Brain That Changes Itself: Stories of Personal Triumph from the Frontiers of Brain Science", 2007.

necessary.

As Eckhart Tolle observed, once you realize that all structures are unstable, peace arises within you.[2] This same truth applies to our careers and identities: embracing that we are always changing, always learning, frees us to continuously reinvent who we are.

Instability isn't the problem. Resisting instability is the problem.

I wrote this book at 48 years old, having just completed my Master's degree in Computer Science with AI/ML specialization while working full-time leading agentic AI initiatives. I got my Bachelor's degree at 46. Not because I'm unusually capable, but because it's never too late to learn what you need to learn.

This book is for those still learning what it means to be fully human in the age of AI: to live with authenticity, boldness, and love—not as passive consumers executing routines, but as beings who grow, adapt, and find meaning in the process of becoming. Whether you're anxious about AI or excited by it, whether you're struggling or thriving, whether you're early in your career or decades in—if you want to understand the pattern that makes technological change navigable, this is your playbook.

The pattern repeats. The playbook works. The question isn't whether you'll survive this transition—it's what you'll build with it.

Let's begin.

Ivan Daunis Llobet
Los Gatos, California
December 2025

---

[2] Tolle, *The Power of Now: A Guide to Spiritual Enlightenment*, 2004.

Contents

PART IV: THRIVING IN THE HYBRID FUTURE   **165**

11 The Career Equation: Judgment × AI   165

12 Building Your "Automation-Proof" Career   185

PART V: THE BIGGER QUESTION   **207**

Chapter 1

The Last Time Humans Were Obsolete

Harvard Observatory, 1880

Edward Charles Pickering had reached his breaking point. The director of Harvard College Observatory stood in his office, fuming at yet another mistake from his male assistant. The calculations were wrong again. The star catalogs were falling behind schedule. In a moment of exasperation, he declared something that would change the course of scientific history: "My maid could do better!"

He wasn't being metaphorical. Pickering hired his maid, Williamina Fleming, to perform astronomical calculations. Within weeks, she proved more capable than the assistant she replaced. Within years, dozens of women filled the observatory's computing rooms, their fingers dancing across adding machines and their minds translating the universe into numbers.

They had a job title that would sound strange to modern ears: they were called "computers."

1.1 The Human Computing Industry

By the early 20th century, human computers had become an essential part of the scientific and military infrastructure.[3] These weren't machines—they were people, mostly women, paid to perform calculations that machines couldn't yet handle.

---

[3] Grier, *When Computers Were Human*, 2005.

1

The work was painstaking and precise. At Harvard, women analyzed photographic plates of stars, measuring brightness and calculating distances. At military ballistics labs, teams computed firing tables for artillery—essential tables that told gunners what angle to aim at different distances, accounting for wind, temperature, and the Earth's rotation. At NASA's precursor organizations, human computers calculated trajectories for aircraft and, eventually, spacecraft. Each calculation required careful attention, each number checked and double-checked, each result recorded in neat handwriting in massive logbooks.

The pay reflected society's view of this work: at Harvard Observatory, women earned twenty-five cents per hour—roughly half what men doing similar work would make. Yet these "computers" were doing genuinely sophisticated mathematics, work that required intelligence, training, and extraordinary attention to detail.

The scale was remarkable. By the 1940s, thousands of human computers worked across the United States. Organizations measured computing capacity not in processing power, but in "kilogirls"—one thousand hours of computing labor. A complex ballistics problem might require ten kilogirls to solve. A major astronomical survey could demand hundreds. During World War II, the need became urgent: every new artillery piece needed firing tables, and those tables required months of calculation.

Among these thousands of computers, a few names would eventually become known.[4] At the National Advisory Committee for Aeronautics (NACA), later NASA, women like Katherine Johnson, Dorothy Vaughan, and Mary Jackson performed calculations that would guide spacecraft and astronauts. But in the 1940s, they were simply doing their jobs, unaware that everything was about to change.

What's striking to me as someone who builds AI systems today is how similar the intellectual challenge was. Human computers weren't just adding numbers—they were pattern matching, error checking, and

---

[4] Shetterly, *Hidden Figures: The American Dream and the Untold Story of the Black Women Mathematicians Who Helped Win the Space Race*, 2016.

developing heuristics to solve problems faster. When a calculation didn't make sense, they'd trace back through their work to find where reality diverged from expectation. Sound familiar? This is exactly what we do when debugging AI systems, when an agent produces an unexpected output and we trace through its reasoning chain to understand what went wrong.

The human computers were, in essence, running algorithms in their minds. They developed shortcuts, optimizations, ways to catch errors before they propagated through entire calculations. Henrietta Leavitt at Harvard discovered the period-luminosity relationship for Cepheid variable stars—not through raw calculation, but by recognizing a pattern that computers (human or electronic) executing rote instructions would have missed. Annie Jump Cannon classified over 350,000 stars by developing a system that balanced precision with efficiency—an optimization problem that would be familiar to any machine learning engineer today.

This wasn't just grunt work. It was intelligent pattern recognition constrained by the speed of human cognition and the limitations of pencil and paper.

1.2   The Crisis Arrives

The change came in the form of ENIAC—the Electronic Numerical Integrator and Computer.[5] Unveiled in 1946 at the University of Pennsylvania, it was massive: thirty tons of equipment filling eighteen hundred square feet, consuming 150 kilowatts of electricity when running. To put that in perspective, ENIAC used as much power as a small neighborhood. When it was turned on, lights across Philadelphia dimmed.

But it could perform five thousand calculations per second—work that would take a human computer weeks.

As an AI engineer who works with GPU clusters daily, these numbers feel oddly familiar. A modern 100-GPU training cluster consumes 30

---

[5] Goldstine and Goldstine, "The ENIAC: First General-Purpose Electronic Computer", 1946.

to 70 kilowatts per hour, depending on the GPU model, plus server overhead. Large AI systems with 64 nodes can draw over 650 kilowatts. The massive GPU farms being built today by companies racing to train frontier models consume megawatts—more power than small towns. We've scaled up the computing power by factors of billions, but we're still grappling with the same fundamental constraint: intelligent computation requires enormous energy.

The goal of ENIAC was explicit and unambiguous: replace human computers entirely. The designers said so plainly. Electronic computers would be faster, more accurate, never tired, and never made arithmetic errors. The business case was clear: one machine could do the work of hundreds of people, with no salary, no benefits, no sick days.

The media seized on this story. *The New York Times* declared that ENIAC could solve in two hours what would take a human computer one hundred years. Business journals predicted massive technological unemployment in computing departments. Defense contractors calculated ROI timelines showing electronic computers would pay for themselves within months. The stock market reacted with enthusiasm—computing equipment manufacturers saw their valuations soar, much like NVIDIA's stock has surged in the current AI boom.

For human computers, the threat was existential. This wasn't about some of their work being automated—it was about their entire profession becoming obsolete. The electronic computer didn't just do calculations faster; it made the very concept of a human computer seem quaint and unnecessary.

The panic was justified. Unlike modern fears about AI that might replace some aspects of knowledge work, this was complete job elimination. There was no ambiguity, no "we'll still need humans for the creative parts." Electronic computers did exactly what human computers did, just faster and cheaper. The job was vanishing.

1.3   What the Experts Got Wrong

But here's what everyone missed, and what I find most relevant to today's AI concerns: they fundamentally misunderstood what "replacement" meant.

The experts in 1946 made the same mistake that many AI analysts make today. They looked at the technology and asked: "Can this machine do what humans do?" When the answer was yes, they concluded: "Then humans are obsolete."

They failed to ask: "What happens when humans no longer need to do this work? What do they do next?"

This is where my experience building AI systems provides a different lens. When we deploy an AI agent that automates a task, we're not eliminating the human—we're freeing them to work on a different level of the problem. The work doesn't disappear; it transforms.

Consider what actually happened with electronic computers. Yes, they could perform calculations faster. But someone had to tell them *what* to calculate. Someone had to set up the problem correctly. Someone had to verify the results made sense. And here's the crucial part: someone had to program the machine.

Programming ENIAC was nothing like programming today. The machine had twenty ten-digit registers—that was its entire memory. To program it, you physically rewired the machine, setting switches and connecting cables. It was tedious, error-prone, and required deep understanding of both the mathematics and the machine's architecture.

Who do you think became the first programmers?

The human computers.[6]

Women like Betty Snyder, Marlyn Wescoff, Ruth Lichterman, Kay McNulty, Betty Jean Jennings, and Fran Bilas—known as the ENIAC Six—were recruited from the human computer ranks to program ENIAC. They weren't chosen because they could write code (the concept barely existed). They were chosen because they understood the problems

---

[6] Light, "When Computers Were Women", 1999.

deeply, because they had developed intuitions about calculations, because they could recognize when results were wrong.

This pattern repeats today in AI development. The best prompt engineers aren't necessarily the people with computer science degrees—they're domain experts who understand the problem space deeply. When I work on fine-tuning large language models, the challenge isn't the code (that's relatively straightforward). The challenge is understanding what the model needs to learn, what examples will teach it effectively, what edge cases matter. It's about programming uncertainty, about coaxing reliable behavior from probabilistic systems.

This feels remarkably similar to what those early programmers faced: trying to squeeze every bit of capability from constrained resources. ENIAC's twenty registers forced extreme optimization. Today, GPU memory constraints force us to use techniques like LoRA and QLoRA—clever mathematical tricks that let us fine-tune massive models without loading all the parameters into memory simultaneously. We're still working within constraints, still innovating to overcome limitations.

1.4   The Trust Problem: Then and Now

But there's another parallel that's even more relevant: the trust problem.

Early electronic computers weren't reliable. ENIAC used seventeen thousand vacuum tubes, and tubes failed constantly. A single failure could corrupt an entire calculation, and you wouldn't necessarily know it happened. The machine might produce a result that looked plausible but was completely wrong.

Sound familiar?

We call it "hallucination" in AI systems—when a language model confidently states something that's completely false. It's the same fundamental problem: a powerful computational system that can't be blindly trusted.

Here's what's fascinating: the solution then was the same as the solution now. You don't eliminate the human—you change their role.

Katherine Johnson, one of the human computers who later became an engineer at NASA, famously verified the electronic computer's calculations for John Glenn's orbital flight.[7] When Glenn was preparing to launch, he insisted: "Get the girl to check the numbers." Not because he thought the computer was wrong, but because he needed human judgment he could trust.

This is exactly how we handle AI hallucinations today: agentic AI systems. An agent doesn't just generate an answer—it verifies its work, uses tools to ground its responses in reality, iteratively refines its output. When an AI agent needs to perform arithmetic, it doesn't try to calculate with tokens (language models are surprisingly bad at math). It calls a calculator tool. When it needs current information, it searches. When it makes a claim, it checks sources.

The human computers became the checkers, the verifiers, the authorities who attested that the machine was correct. They moved up the stack from executing calculations to ensuring correctness. Today, we're seeing the same shift: from writing every line of code to reviewing AI-generated code, from performing analysis to validating AI analysis, from executing tasks to orchestrating AI agents.

1.5   A Technical Parallel: Computer Vision

There's another historical parallel that illuminates what's happening today, and it's more recent: computer vision before deep learning.

For twenty years, from roughly 1990 to 2010, computer vision researchers made steady, incremental progress using hand-crafted features. Algorithms like SIFT (Scale-Invariant Feature Transform), HOG (Histogram of Oriented Gradients), and dozens of others represented the state of the art. Researchers spent careers developing these heuristics, each providing small improvements in accuracy.

This was remarkably similar to what human computers did: developing sophisticated manual techniques to solve problems that seemed

[7] Shetterly, *Hidden Figures: The American Dream and the Untold Story of the Black Women Mathematicians Who Helped Win the Space Race*, 2016.

to require human intelligence. Each new feature detector was like a new calculation method—a clever way to extract signal from noise.

Then, in 2012, deep learning arrived.[8] Convolutional neural networks trained on ImageNet[9] didn't just improve on hand-crafted features— they made them obsolete overnight. Twenty years of careful research became largely irrelevant. The improvement wasn't incremental; it was a phase transition.

Did this make computer vision researchers obsolete? No. But it completely transformed what they did. Instead of crafting features by hand, they designed network architectures, curated datasets, developed training strategies. The work became more about understanding what the machine needed to learn rather than doing the learning themselves.

This is the same transformation that human computers underwent. The work didn't disappear—it moved to a higher level of abstraction.

1.6   Why This Time Feels Different (But Isn't)

I hear the objection: "But AI is different. It's not just replacing calculation—it's replacing thinking."

Is it, though? What were human computers doing if not thinking? They were pattern matching, error checking, optimizing algorithms in their heads. When we say "thinking," we often mean exactly these activities.

Here's what I've learned building AI systems: the more sophisticated the AI becomes, the more sophisticated the human work becomes. Not less sophisticated—more.

When I work with large language models, I'm not competing with them on speed or breadth of knowledge. I'm doing something the model can't: I'm deciding what problems matter, what approaches make sense given business constraints, what risks are acceptable, what the second-order effects might be.

---

[8] Krizhevsky, Sutskever, and Hinton, "ImageNet Classification with Deep Convolutional Neural Networks", 2012.

[9] Deng et al., "ImageNet: A Large-Scale Hierarchical Image Database", 2009.

This is exactly what happened to human computers. As machines took over calculation, human work shifted to problems that required judgment, context, creativity. Problems that were intellectually more challenging, more interesting, more rewarding.

And here's the key insight: people who loved being human computers loved solving problems. When given the opportunity to solve harder, more interesting problems using more powerful tools, most of them jumped at it. They didn't want to just repeat calculations—they wanted intellectual challenge. Programming computers, designing systems, advancing science—these were more appealing than calculating firing tables by hand.

Today's software engineers are the same. We're not motivated by typing characters into files. We're motivated by solving problems, by building systems that work, by understanding complex domains. When AI handles the routine coding, we get to focus on the interesting parts: architecture, tradeoffs, business logic, edge cases that require judgment.

The form of work changed. The motivation didn't.

1.7 Government Investment: Then and Now

There's one more parallel worth exploring: government funding.

ENIAC was built with military funding during World War II. The explicit goal was national security—computing firing tables faster meant better artillery, which meant winning the war. After the war, government investment continued. The space race drove massive investment in computing. The Department of Defense funded early computer science research. National laboratories pushed the boundaries of what machines could do.

Today, we're seeing the same pattern. DARPA funds AI research explicitly for national security applications. The Department of Energy invests in AI for scientific computing. Nations compete to build sovereign AI capabilities. The rhetoric is identical: AI supremacy equals economic and military advantage.

The difference is scale. The U.S. government spent roughly $500,000 to build ENIAC (about $8 million in today's dollars). Current estimates suggest the U.S. government will spend tens of billions on AI research and infrastructure over the next decade. Private sector investment dwarfs even that.

But the pattern is the same: transformative technology driven by national priorities, with civilian applications following military investment.

What happened after ENIAC? The computing industry exploded. By 1970, there were 150,000 computer programmers in the United States[10]—thirty times more than there had been human computers in 1950. By 2020, over four million people worked in software development.[11]

The jobs didn't disappear. They multiplied.

1.8   The Messy Middle: 1946-1960

History books make the transition seem clean: human computers, then electronic computers, then programmers. But the reality was messier and more interesting.

For years, human computers and electronic computers worked side by side. The machines handled large-scale calculations, but humans still verified results, set up problems, and handled edge cases. Gradually, as machines became more reliable and programming techniques improved, the balance shifted.

Some human computers transitioned successfully. Many became programmers, systems analysts, or moved into management. They brought invaluable domain knowledge—understanding the problems deeply enough to know what the machines should calculate.

Others struggled. Some were older and found learning programming daunting. Some were in organizations that didn't invest in retraining.

---

[10] U.S. Bureau of Labor Statistics, *Computing Occupations Historical Data*, 1970.

[11] U.S. Census Bureau, *Computer and Information Technology Occupations*, 2014.

Some simply didn't want to change—they liked what they did and didn't see why they should have to learn something new.

This variation in outcomes is crucial to understand. Technological transformation creates opportunities, but it doesn't guarantee success for everyone. Those who adapted early, who learned new skills, who saw the machines as tools rather than threats—they thrived. Those who resisted or lacked opportunities struggled.

The same thing is happening today with AI. Some engineers are diving deep into prompt engineering, fine-tuning, agentic systems. They're learning to work with AI rather than competing against it. Others are dismissing AI as hype or hoping it goes away. In ten years, we'll see vastly different outcomes for these two groups.

1.9   The Adaptation Pattern

If you're reading this book, you're probably not a human computer in 1946. But you might be a knowledge worker in 2025 wondering if AI will make you obsolete.

The human computer story reveals a pattern—one I've seen repeat across every wave of technological change I've lived through. I call it **The Adaptation Pattern**, and it consists of five principles that have held true for over a century:

Principle 1: The Power Principle

Technology will be more powerful than you expect.

ENIAC really did make human calculation obsolete. Modern AI really is impressive, and it's improving exponentially. Every technological wave has exceeded initial predictions of capability. Dismissing new technology as hype is consistently wrong.

Don't bet against the technology. It will be more capable than skeptics claim.

11

Principle 2: The Transformation Principle

"Replacement" means transformation, not elimination.

The work transforms—it doesn't disappear. When human computers were "replaced," what actually happened was that work evolved to a higher level of abstraction. New roles emerged that required human judgment, creativity, and understanding. The total number of jobs increased, not decreased.

Your work will change. It won't vanish.

Principle 3: The Early Mover Principle

Those who adapt early gain compounding advantages.

The human computers who learned programming in the late 1940s had twenty-year careers ahead of them. Those who waited until the 1960s faced a much steeper climb. Early adoption gives you years of experience while others are still deciding whether to start.

Time is the resource you can't buy back. Start now.

Principle 4: The Messy Middle Principle

Transitions are uncertain and unfair—but navigable.

There's no guarantee of smooth sailing. Success depends on your adaptability, your organization's support, and sometimes factors outside your control. Some people will struggle despite doing everything right. The transition period is genuinely difficult.

But the overall direction is clear: humans move up the value chain. The mess is temporary. The transformation is permanent.

Principle 5: The Human Core Principle

Human value shifts to what machines can't do.

The pioneers who thrived weren't better calculators than ENIAC. They brought understanding, judgment, creativity, and the ability to bridge between problems and solutions. AI can generate code; it can't decide what's worth building. It can analyze data; it can't determine what the data means. It can optimize processes; it can't define what success looks like.

Focus on what you uniquely bring. That's where your value remains.

These five principles—Power, Transformation, Early Mover, Messy Middle, and Human Core—form the Adaptation Pattern. It's not a theory I invented. It's a pattern I observed in history and confirmed through personal experience. Every chapter that follows will show you how to apply it.

The question isn't whether you'll be replaced. The question is: will you adapt?

The human computers did. Most of them thrived. The ones who became programmers, who learned to work with machines rather than compete against them, who moved to higher-level thinking—they had rewarding careers doing more interesting work than they'd done before.

That's the real lesson from 1946. Not that humans became obsolete, but that humans evolved. And in that evolution lies our path forward.

The next chapter explores what actually happened to those human computers. Spoiler: the outcome was far more positive than anyone in 1946 predicted. Understanding why their predictions were wrong is the key to understanding why today's AI doom predictions are likely wrong as well.

Chapter 2

What Actually Happened

University of Pennsylvania, 1945

Betty Snyder stood in front of ENIAC for the first time, staring at eighteen thousand vacuum tubes, seventy thousand resistors, and enough wiring to make even the most experienced electrical engineer's head spin. She'd been pulled from her job as a human computer calculating artillery trajectories to do something nobody had a name for yet. The machine was built. Someone needed to make it work.

"Program it," they said, as if that explained anything.

There was no manual. No programming language. No one had ever programmed a computer before because no one had ever needed to. To make ENIAC solve a ballistics problem, you physically rewired the machine, setting thousands of switches and connecting hundreds of cables in exactly the right sequence. Get one wrong, and nothing worked.

Betty and five other women—the ENIAC Six—figured it out. They weren't chosen because they knew how to code. They were chosen because they understood the problems deeply. They'd spent months calculating trajectories by hand. They knew when an answer made sense and when it didn't. They could think through the logic of computation because they'd been doing it in their heads.

The women who were supposedly being replaced by ENIAC became the first people to program it.

This shouldn't have been possible according to the predictions.

Human computers were obsolete. The machines had won. Yet here were human computers doing something the machines couldn't do at all: figuring out what problems to solve and how to solve them.

2.1 The Pattern Emerges

What happened to Betty Snyder and the other ENIAC programmers wasn't an exception. It was the beginning of a pattern that would repeat across the entire computing industry for the next two decades.

The first official Census data on computing occupations came in 1970, when the Census Bureau finally recognized "computer workers" as a distinct category. By then, 450,000 people worked in information technology—a number that included programmers, systems analysts, and computer specialists. This was in an era when computers still filled entire rooms and cost millions of dollars.

By 1980, that number had grown to 781,000 workers, a 74 percent increase in just one decade. By 1990, 1.5 million people worked in IT. The year 2000 saw 3.4 million IT workers, and by 2014, 4.6 million Americans worked in information technology occupations.[12]

Let me put that in perspective. In the late 1940s, thousands of human computers worked across the United States. By 2014, the computing industry employed more than four and a half million people—a thousandfold increase in total employment.

The jobs didn't disappear. They multiplied.

But raw numbers don't tell the full story. What matters is what happened to the people—the human computers who faced an existential threat to their profession. Did they end up unemployed? Did they become obsolete?

No. Many of them became the pioneers of the software industry.

---

[12] U.S. Census Bureau, *Computer and Information Technology Occupations*, 2014.

2.2 Grace Hopper's Revolution

Grace Hopper started her career as a mathematician and human computer.[13] She'd joined the Naval Reserve during World War II and was assigned to the Bureau of Ordnance Computation Project at Harvard. There, she worked on the Mark I computer, one of the earliest electromechanical computers.

When the war ended, most women were expected to return home. Hopper stayed in computing. She joined the team developing UNIVAC, one of the first commercial computers. And she had a radical idea: programming was too hard.

This might seem obvious now, but in the late 1940s, it was unorthodox. Programming meant manipulating binary code, setting switches, connecting wires. It was technical work that required understanding the machine's architecture at the deepest level. The assumption was that this was just how programming would always be.

Hopper thought differently. She'd spent years doing calculations by hand. She knew that the hard part wasn't the calculation itself—it was understanding what needed to be calculated and why. She believed that programmers should be able to write instructions in something closer to human language, and let the computer translate those instructions into machine code.

She invented the compiler—a program that translates human-readable code into machine instructions. This was revolutionary. It meant that programmers no longer needed to think like machines. They could think like mathematicians, scientists, engineers. They could focus on solving problems rather than manipulating bits.

Her work culminated in COBOL, one of the first high-level programming languages. COBOL wasn't designed for computer scientists. It was designed for business people, for accountants, for anyone who needed to solve problems with computers but didn't want to become an electrical engineer first.

---

[13] Hopper, *The Education of a Computer*, 1952.

Hopper retired from the Navy as a Rear Admiral. She gave speeches, taught at universities, mentored young programmers. The human computer who was supposed to become obsolete instead revolutionized how we program computers.

The pattern here is crucial: Hopper didn't compete with the machine on the machine's terms. She didn't try to calculate faster than UNIVAC. Instead, she moved to a higher level of abstraction. She focused on the problem that humans were uniquely suited to solve: making computers accessible to other humans.

2.3 Margaret Hamilton and the Birth of Software Engineering

Margaret Hamilton's story follows a similar arc, but two decades later, when computers had evolved significantly.[14]

Hamilton started as a mathematician. In 1960, she took a job at MIT programming software to predict weather patterns. This was still early in computing history. Software engineering as a discipline didn't exist yet. There were programmers, but programming was seen as a support function, something you did to make the hardware work.

Hamilton saw it differently. She believed that software was as critical as hardware—maybe more critical. When NASA needed software for the Apollo program, Hamilton led the effort. She wasn't just writing code; she was inventing the processes and practices that would define software engineering as a profession.

Her team developed the flight software that guided Apollo 11 to the moon. During the landing, the computer's alarms started going off—it was being overloaded with data. The astronauts wanted to abort. Mission Control wasn't sure. Hamilton's software handled it. The system prioritized critical tasks, ignored non-essential inputs, and brought the lunar module down safely.

That software saved the mission. More than that, it demonstrated

---

[14] Hamilton, "Apollo Flight Software Development", 1971.

something fundamental: software isn't just instructions for a machine. It's a critical system that requires rigorous engineering, testing, and design. Hamilton popularized the term "software engineering" to elevate the discipline, to make people understand that building reliable software required the same rigor as building bridges or spacecraft.

The woman who started as a mathematician became the director of MIT's Software Engineering Division. She founded her own software company. She received the Presidential Medal of Freedom in 2016 for her contributions to Apollo and to software engineering as a field.

Hamilton's story illustrates another crucial pattern: the human computers who thrived didn't just learn to use the new tools. They defined how those tools should be used. They created the methodologies, the best practices, the entire conceptual framework for working with computers.

2.4   When Humans Verify Machines

The transition from human to electronic computers also revealed something profound about trust and accountability.

As we explored in Chapter 1, astronauts trusted human verification of computer calculations even when the computers were faster and more accurate. This wasn't about capability—it was about understanding, judgment, and the ability to explain why results made sense. Electronic computers calculated; humans provided the understanding and accountability that made those calculations trustworthy.

This pattern of humans moving from execution to verification and oversight became fundamental to how computing evolved. The people who had been doing the calculations became the authorities who ensured the machines were correct.

2.5   The Five-Stage Pattern

Looking at these stories and hundreds of others like them, a clear pattern emerges. The transition from human computers to electronic computers followed five predictable stages:

Stage 1: Machines took over routine calculations. ENIAC could compute firing tables faster than any human.[15] This was indisputable, undeniable, and exactly what everyone feared. The core task that defined the human computer profession became automated.

Stage 2: Humans moved to programming the machines. Someone had to tell the computers what to calculate. This required understanding both the problem domain and the machine's capabilities. The human computers, who understood the problems deeply, were ideally positioned for this work.[16] Betty Snyder and the ENIAC Six weren't hired despite being human computers; they were hired *because* they were human computers.

Stage 3: New roles emerged that didn't exist before. As programming developed, entirely new occupations appeared. Systems analysts who translated business problems into technical requirements. Software engineers who designed reliable, maintainable systems. Computer scientists who pushed the theoretical boundaries of computation. Compilers, operating systems, databases, networks—each innovation created new types of work that required human expertise.

Stage 4: Total employment in computing exploded. From thousands of human computers in the 1940s to 450,000 IT workers in 1970[17] to 4.6 million in 2014.[18] Every prediction about technological unemployment was wrong. The computing industry didn't just grow; it became one of the largest employment sectors in the economy.

Stage 5: The work became more valuable and intellectually rewarding. Human computers earned twenty-five cents an hour at Harvard in the 1940s—half what men made for similar work. By 2014, IT workers earned a median of $80,895 for men and $70,385 for women, significantly above the median for all occupations. More importantly, the work involved solving complex problems, creating new systems, pushing

---

[15] Goldstine and Goldstine, "The ENIAC: First General-Purpose Electronic Computer", 1946.

[16] Light, "When Computers Were Women", 1999.

[17] U.S. Bureau of Labor Statistics, *Computing Occupations Historical Data*, 1970.

[18] U.S. Census Bureau, *Computer and Information Technology Occupations*, 2014.

the boundaries of what was possible. The pioneers established entirely new fields and contributed to achievements from space exploration to the foundations of the digital age.

This pattern didn't just happen once. It repeated across every sector where computers were introduced, across every decade from the 1950s onward.

2.6   Why the Predictions Were Wrong

The experts who predicted mass unemployment made a fundamental error. They saw computers as replacements when they were actually amplifiers.

We see this same error being made today with AI. When people say "AI will replace programmers," they're making the same mistake the experts made in 1946. They're looking at specific tasks—writing code, debugging, testing—and asking, "Can AI do this?" When the answer is yes, they conclude that programmers will become obsolete.

But that's not how it works. Let me explain using an analogy from modern software development.

When I write code today, I don't write assembly language. I don't manually manage memory allocation. I don't handle low-level network protocols. Compilers, interpreters, frameworks, and libraries automate all of this for me. These tools do work that used to require human programmers.

Did those tools eliminate programming jobs? No. They enabled programmers to build vastly more complex systems. A modern web application involves thousands of components that would have been impossible to build in assembly language. The automation didn't eliminate the work; it raised the level of abstraction.

This is exactly what happened with human computers. Electronic computers automated calculation. But calculation was never the end goal—it was a means to an end. Scientists didn't want ballistics tables because they loved tables. They wanted to aim artillery accurately.

They didn't want orbital trajectories because math was fun. They wanted to send humans to space.

Once computers automated the calculation part, people could focus on the actual problems: What should we calculate? How do we verify the results? What do these numbers tell us about reality? How do we translate complex problems into computable models?

These questions required judgment, creativity, domain knowledge, and intuition—exactly what humans provide and machines don't.

2.7 The Modern Parallel: What We're Seeing Now

The same pattern is unfolding today with AI, and I see it daily in my work.

We've built systems that automate software development tasks. They can generate code, write tests, analyze logs, suggest optimizations. Tasks that used to take engineers days now happen in hours. If you looked at this and asked, "Can AI do what developers do?" you'd conclude that developers are at risk.

But that's not what's happening. Instead, we're seeing the exact pattern that happened with human computers:

Machines are taking over routine tasks. AI agents handle boilerplate code, repetitive patterns, standard test cases. They're good at this. Better than humans, in many cases.

Engineers are moving to higher-level work. Instead of writing CRUD operations for the hundredth time, engineers focus on architecture decisions, business logic, edge cases that require judgment. They're prompting the AI, reviewing its output, integrating its work into larger systems.

New roles are emerging. We now have engineers who specialize in prompt engineering, who design agent workflows, who evaluate AI-generated code for security and maintainability. These jobs didn't exist two years ago.

We're building bigger systems faster. The AI doesn't reduce how much we can build; it expands it. Projects that would have required ten engineers can now be done by five engineers with AI assistance. But we're not firing five engineers. We're taking on twice as many projects.

The work is more interesting. Nobody joined software engineering because they loved writing boilerplate code. They joined to solve problems, build systems that matter, create things that didn't exist before. AI handles the tedious parts. Engineers focus on the creative parts.

The engineers who thrive with AI systems share specific characteristics, and they're the same characteristics that helped human computers transition successfully:

They embrace the new tools instead of resisting them. They learn how to work with AI rather than competing against it. They focus on problems that require judgment and creativity. They understand that their value comes from knowing what to build and why, not from typing characters into files.

The engineers who struggle are the ones who see AI as a threat, who refuse to learn the new tools, who define their value by the mechanics of implementation rather than the quality of solutions.

2.8   The Failures: What We Can Learn

But let's be honest about something the success stories often gloss over: not everyone made the transition successfully.

Some human computers never became programmers. Some found the new work too technical, too different from what they knew. Some were in organizations that didn't invest in retraining. Some were older workers facing age discrimination in a field that increasingly valued youth. Some were simply in the wrong place at the wrong time.

We don't know exact numbers because people who failed to transition didn't make it into the history books. But we know they existed. When the University of Pennsylvania's Moore School needed programmers for ENIAC, they chose six women out of dozens of human computers. What happened to the others?

Some found other work. Some left the workforce. Some struggled. The transition wasn't smooth or guaranteed for everyone.

The same pattern holds today. Not every engineer successfully adopts AI tools. Some are in companies that expect them to compete with AI rather than collaborate with it. Some face age bias in an industry obsessed with youth. Some lack access to training or opportunities to learn new skills.

The lesson here is crucial: technological transformation creates opportunities, but it doesn't guarantee success for everyone. The outcomes depend on individual adaptability, organizational support, and sometimes just luck.

This is why building skills before you need them matters so much. The human computers who transitioned successfully to programming had often been seeking opportunities to learn about electronic computers before they needed those skills. Dorothy Vaughan taught herself FORTRAN programming at night, preparing for a change she saw coming. When NASA needed programmers, she was ready.

Today's engineers who are thriving with AI are those who started experimenting with GPT-3 when it was just a curiosity, who learned prompt engineering before it was a job requirement, who built side projects with AI tools before their employers required it.

2.9 The Caveat About AI Companies

There's an important caveat here. If you're working at an AI company building foundational models, your trajectory might look different from the historical pattern.

Companies building AI infrastructure face unique risks. The technology evolves rapidly. What seems like a competitive advantage today can become obsolete in months. Investment cycles drive boom-and-bust patterns. Companies that look unstoppable can collapse when funding dries up or when a competitor releases a better model.

I've seen this personally. Early adopters of GPT-3 built elaborate systems for agentic AI, investing months of engineering effort. Then GPT-4 arrived with function calling and better reasoning, making much of that work obsolete. Then GPT-4o came out. Then GPT-4.5. Each iteration required rebuilding systems that had just been completed.

The companies that will thrive are those building on top of AI rather than merely wrapping it. They're solving problems that require domain expertise, integration with existing systems, human judgment about when and how to use AI. They're using AI as a tool to build something valuable rather than treating AI itself as the product.

This mirrors what happened with human computers. The companies that thrived were those that used electronic computers to solve real problems—aerospace, weather prediction, scientific research, business operations. The companies that failed were those that simply replaced human computers with machines without changing anything else about how they worked.

2.10   What "Thriving" Actually Means

When we say the human computers thrived, what do we mean?

On one level, it's straightforward: career advancement and compensation. The pioneers achieved positions and prestige far exceeding what they would have as human computers, with earnings and influence that reflected their contributions to foundational technologies.

But material success isn't the full story. These pioneers describe their work with a sense of intellectual fulfillment that's striking when you read their interviews and memoirs. They weren't just earning paychecks; they were solving problems that mattered, creating things that didn't exist before, pushing the boundaries of what was possible.

Hamilton talks about the satisfaction of seeing her code guide astronauts to the moon. Hopper speaks with excitement about making programming accessible to people who weren't computer scientists. Others describe the thrill of working on missions that expanded human knowledge.

This is what thriving means: doing work that challenges you intellectually, that makes a difference, that gives you agency in shaping the future. It's not just about money or status, though those matter. It's about the quality of the work itself.

We see the same pattern in engineers today who work effectively with AI. They're not just more productive or better compensated (though many are). They describe their work as more interesting, more focused on the problems they care about, less bogged down in tedium. They're building systems they couldn't have built before, solving problems that seemed intractable, creating innovations that were impossible without AI assistance.

The impact on society matters too. The human computers and the programmers who followed them built the foundation for the digital age. The software running in spacecraft, weather forecasting systems, business operations, scientific research—all of it traces back to the work of people who started as human computers and evolved with the technology.

Today's engineers working with AI are shaping how artificial intelligence integrates into society. The decisions they make about what to automate and what to keep human, how to design AI systems that augment rather than replace human judgment, how to build tools that are useful rather than just impressive—these decisions will matter for decades.

Thriving means having agency in this transformation rather than being passive victims of it.

2.11   The Uncomfortable Truth

Here's something that makes people uncomfortable: the transition was messy, it wasn't fair, and it required significant adaptation from the workers who succeeded.

The human computers had to learn entirely new skills. They had to start over in many ways, moving from calculation to programming, from following procedures to designing systems. This was hard work. Some of them never fully mastered it. Some struggled for years. Some would have preferred to keep doing what they were doing.

The fair thing would have been for employers to invest heavily in retraining, to provide extended support, to guarantee employment during the transition. Some employers did this. Many didn't. The outcomes varied dramatically based on factors the workers couldn't control—which organization they worked for, which supervisors they had, what opportunities were available.

We're seeing the same unfairness today. Some engineers work for companies that invest in AI training, provide time to learn new tools, create opportunities to work on AI-enhanced projects. Others work for companies that simply expect them to figure it out on their own while maintaining full productivity in their current roles.

This isn't right. But it's reality. The question for any individual worker isn't what should happen in an ideal world. It's what to do given the world as it is.

The human computers who thrived were those who took responsibility for their own adaptation. Dorothy Vaughan didn't wait for NASA to offer FORTRAN training. She taught herself. Grace Hopper didn't wait for someone to invent high-level programming languages. She invented them herself.

This is a tension in the book that I want to be honest about. On one hand, I believe companies have a responsibility to support their workers through technological transitions. On the other hand, I know that many companies won't live up to that responsibility. The practical advice for any individual is: don't wait for your employer to save you. Build skills before you need them. Adapt proactively rather than reactively.

2.12　The Pattern Confirmed

The human computer story confirms every principle of the Adaptation Pattern we identified in Chapter 1.

The Power Principle: Electronic computers exceeded all predictions. They didn't just match human calculation—they made it obsolete within a decade.

The Transformation Principle: The work didn't disappear. It multiplied. From thousands of human computers to millions of programmers, engineers, and IT professionals. Total employment grew by orders of magnitude.

The Early Mover Principle: Dorothy Vaughan taught herself FORTRAN before NASA offered training. Grace Hopper invented compilers while others were still learning to program. The pioneers who moved first had decades of advantage.

The Messy Middle Principle: The transition was unfair. Some organizations retrained workers; others didn't. Success depended partly on factors workers couldn't control. But those who took responsibility for their own adaptation fared better than those who waited.

The Human Core Principle: The pioneers who thrived weren't better calculators than ENIAC. They brought judgment about what to calculate, creativity in how to solve problems, and the ability to make machines useful for human purposes.

The question isn't whether you'll be replaced. The question is whether you'll adapt.

The human computers did. Most of them thrived. The ones who became programmers, who learned to work with machines rather than compete against them, who moved to higher-level thinking—they had rewarding careers doing more interesting, more impactful work than they'd done before.

That's not just history. It's the playbook for today.

The next chapter explores my personal journey through multiple waves of supposed obsolescence. Each time, the Adaptation Pattern repeated. Each time, those who recognized it early thrived. And each time, the work became more valuable and more human, not less.

Chapter 3

A Personal History of "Obsolescence"

Barcelona, 1992

I was fifteen, staring at a problem that seemed impossible. A shoe manufacturing company needed an accounting system. I knew C++— I'd been teaching myself for a year, reading Bjarne Stroustrup's books, writing little programs that did mostly nothing useful. C++ felt like the future. Object-oriented programming, templates, the whole elegant architecture of it.

But here's the thing: building an accounting system in C++ would take months. I only had a few weeks left of my school break, and the company needed it yesterday.

Antonio—a friend of my mother's who had taken me under his wing—said, "Learn Clipper."

Clipper? It was this weird database language that felt ancient even then. But it had libraries for everything—forms, reports, data tables. Everything I needed was already there. I could learn it in a few weeks and ship something that worked.

I had a choice: stick with the language I loved, or learn the tool that solved the problem.

I learned Clipper. Built the accounting system. Shipped it.

That's when I realized something fundamental about this industry: the skill isn't mastering one technology. The skill is recognizing when to abandon what you know and learn what you need.

I've been doing that ever since.

3.1 Wave 1: The Tools That Replace Us (1990s-2000s)

3.1.1 Building the Automators

By the late 1990s, I was building shareware in Barcelona. Image viewers, format conversion tools, utilities that did one thing really well. This was before app stores, before SaaS. You'd build something, upload it to download sites, hope someone would register it for $20.

I created tools like Hyper Clouds for designers, Gif2Swf for converting animated GIFs to Flash. These were small utilities, but they solved real problems. Gif2Swf got featured on Chris Pirillo's LockerGnome podcast—suddenly thousands of people were downloading it. For a kid in Barcelona, seeing download counters tick up from across the Atlantic felt like magic.

Here's what's funny: I was building automation tools. Gif2Swf took something that required hand-animating in Flash and made it automatic. Click, convert, done. I was literally building software that replaced manual work.

But I didn't see it as replacement. I saw it as amplification. Designers could try fifty variations instead of three. They could experiment faster, iterate more, focus on creativity instead of tedious frame-by-frame work.

The irony wouldn't become clear until later: I was building the exact kind of tool that people now fear AI will become.

3.1.2 The Year 2000: Terrible Timing, Perfect Education

In 2000, I moved from Barcelona to the United States to start my own company. The dot-com bubble was imploding. NASDAQ was crashing. Startups were dying by the hundreds.

Fantastic timing, right?

But here's what I learned: crashes create opportunities if you're paying attention. Everyone else was running away from internet companies. I was walking in. Bandwidth costs were dropping. Server prices were falling. The infrastructure for what I wanted to build—streaming video, web applications, multimedia tools—was finally becoming viable.

I joined Sausage Software in Blaine, Washington. They made HotDog, a web editor that competed with Dreamweaver and FrontPage. The beautiful irony: I was working on a tool that people said would make hand-coding obsolete, while hand-coding everything myself.

We built web editors. WYSIWYG interfaces. Drag-and-drop components. Tools that were supposed to eliminate the need for programmers.

Did they? No. They eliminated the need for programmers who only knew how to write HTML tags. But they created demand for people who understood *why* you'd structure a page one way versus another, who could build components that non-programmers could use, who could make tools that were actually useful instead of just technically impressive.

I contributed to HotDog Professional, worked on Flashpoint, built plugins for Viewpoint's 3D media player. Each project taught me the same lesson: automation doesn't eliminate the job. It raises the abstraction level.

When HotDog could generate a form automatically, the question stopped being "how do I write form HTML?" and became "what form should this page have?" That's a harder question. A more valuable question.

3.1.3   The Pattern Emerges

By the mid-2000s, I'd seen this pattern repeat a dozen times. Every new framework, every automation tool, every library that made something "easy"—people would panic. "This will replace developers!"

It never did.

What happened instead: the boring parts got automated, and we moved to more interesting problems. Before jQuery, I wrote hundreds of lines of JavaScript to handle cross-browser compatibility. After jQuery, I wrote ten lines and spent my time solving actual user problems.

Before content management systems, I hand-coded every page. After CMS platforms, I built systems that let non-technical people manage their own content while I focused on architecture and performance.

Each wave felt like it might be the one that made me obsolete. Each wave actually made me more valuable, because I learned the new tools while understanding the problems they solved.

Think about it this way: automation is like a rising tide. You can stand still and drown, or you can learn to swim at the new water level. The water keeps rising. That's not changing. Your choice is whether to rise with it.

3.2   Wave 2: Infrastructure Disappears (2000s-2010s)

3.2.1   The Data Center Days

In the mid-2000s, if you wanted to run a web application, you bought physical servers. Not cloud instances—actual machines. You'd spec them out, order them, wait for delivery, drive to a data center in San Jose, rack them yourself, configure everything by hand.

I remember carrying servers into data centers. Heavy Dell boxes that cost thousands of dollars each. Setting up Apache, MySQL, configuring networks, managing firewalls. If you had high traffic, it was a nightmare. You'd need load balancers, backup servers, redundant storage. The capital costs were enormous.

For startups, this was existential. You needed tens of thousands of dollars just to launch. If you succeeded and traffic spiked, you'd scramble to buy more servers, wait for delivery, hope you could scale fast enough.

3.2.2   The S3 Moment

In 2007, I was running Use Labs, building video streaming platforms for local TV stations. Storage was killing us. Video files are huge. Bandwidth is expensive. We were constantly calculating: how many servers do we need? How much storage? What if traffic spikes?

Then AWS S3 launched.[19] Cloud storage that you paid for by the gigabyte. No upfront costs. No servers to buy. No data centers to manage.

Almost nobody was using it yet. People didn't trust putting their data on "someone else's computers." Security concerns. Reliability worries. What if Amazon shut it down?

I tried it anyway. Started small, tested it, moved more and more data to S3. It was a phase transition. Suddenly storage wasn't a capital expense—it was an operating expense that scaled with usage. We could store terabytes of video without buying a single server.

The competitive advantage was immediate. Other companies were still buying storage arrays. We were paying pennies per gigabyte and scaling infinitely.

Here's what I learned: being an early adopter of infrastructure automation gives you years of advantage. By the time everyone else figured out S3 was reliable, we'd built entire systems around it. We understood its limitations, knew how to optimize costs, had architectural patterns that competitors were just discovering.

3.2.3   The 2008 Crisis: Adaptation Under Pressure

Then 2008 hit. Financial crisis. Credit froze. Our customers—local TV stations—stopped spending. Not reduced spending. Stopped.

We were saving them millions with our streaming platform. Didn't matter. They had zero budget for anything new. Projects we'd been working on for months got cancelled overnight.

We had a choice: keep trying to sell enterprise video streaming into a frozen market, or pivot.

We pivoted. Started building content management systems for small businesses. Smaller deals, faster sales cycles, customers who could still spend a few thousand dollars. Not as exciting as streaming video, but it paid the bills.

Was this adapting up the value chain? Not really. It was adapting

---

[19] Amazon Web Services, *Amazon S3 Launch*, 2006.

to market conditions. Sometimes survival requires moving sideways, not up.

But here's what I gained: I learned how to build systems fast. CMS platforms taught me templating, content modeling, user management at scale. Skills that would matter later, even if they felt like a step backward at the time.

3.2.4 Puppet to Docker: The Automation Cascade

Infrastructure automation kept accelerating. We'd started using Puppet for server configuration—write code that describes what servers should look like, and Puppet makes it happen. No more manual SSH sessions, no more configuration drift.

I spent months learning Puppet. Built our entire deployment system around it. Got really good at it.

Then Docker arrived. Containers that packaged applications with all their dependencies. Suddenly Puppet's approach—configure servers, then deploy code—felt obsolete. With Docker, the container *was* the configuration.

This felt different. Puppet hadn't been around that long. I'd just invested significant time mastering it. Now this new thing was making it irrelevant?

But Docker was clearly better. Faster deployments, more consistent environments, easier rollbacks. Fighting it would be stupid.

So I learned Docker. Then Kubernetes. Then Terraform for infrastructure as code. Each tool made the previous generation obsolete faster than the last.

The half-life of infrastructure tools kept shrinking. What used to take five years now took two. But the pattern remained: those who learned the new tools early had an advantage. Those who waited struggled.

3.3 Wave 3: The Resistance (2010s-2020)

3.3.1 The Control Problem

By the 2010s, I'd reached a weird place psychologically. I was a senior engineer. I knew how everything worked—networking, databases, algorithms, systems architecture. I could build anything from scratch.

And that became a problem.

Libraries and frameworks kept getting better. MapReduce and Spark for distributed processing. SciKit-learn for machine learning. React for front-end development. Each tool solved problems I knew how to solve manually.

I started making excuses. "That library is too slow." "The license isn't permissive enough." "I don't trust the security."

Those were rationalizations. The real reason: I felt that I needed full control. Using libraries felt like admitting I couldn't do it myself. Like I was becoming less valuable.

This is the trap senior engineers fall into. We confuse our value with our ability to implement everything from scratch. We resist tools because they feel like threats to our expertise.

Here's the thing: I was fighting against the same pattern I'd seen succeed four times already. But when it's happening to *you*, when it's *your* skills feeling obsolete, rationality goes out the window.

3.3.2 Jetlore: The Credential Gap

In 2016, I joined Jetlore, a machine learning startup doing recommendation systems for e-commerce. We built sophisticated algorithms—collaborative filtering, clustering, personalized ranking. Real ML at scale.

PayPal acquired Jetlore. Perfect, right? Now I'd be doing ML at a major tech company.

Except their ML teams wanted PhDs. Or at least master's degrees in data science. Formal credentials that proved you understood the mathematics, the theory, the academic foundations.

I had twenty years of software engineering experience. I'd built recommendation systems. I'd implemented clustering algorithms in Scala. I understood the work.

But I didn't have the credentials. No bachelor's degree in computer science. No master's in machine learning. Just experience.

The organization wasn't ready to embrace ML broadly yet anyway—this was 2016, before the current AI boom. But I could see where things were heading. ML was going to be huge. And I'd be locked out unless I repositioned myself.

So I left. Not because the company wasn't ready for ML. Because *I* wasn't credentialed for the future I saw coming.

3.3.3 The Learning Years: 2019-2024

What followed was deliberate. I worked at RetailNext, Deloitte, Clovers AI, Evolv AI. Each role deepened different aspects of ML and AI: computer vision and multi-cloud deployment, real-time recommendation systems, video processing and transcription, generative AI and deep learning.

But I was also doing something else: building the credentials I lacked.

In 2018, I took Stanford's Machine Learning course on Coursera. Then deeplearning.ai's deep learning specialization. Every certification I could find. Building a portfolio that said "yes, I understand this formally, not just practically."

In 2023, at 46 years old, I enrolled at Western Governors University to get my Bachelor's in Computer Science. While working full-time. While building production ML systems.

People thought I was crazy. "You've been a software engineer for twenty-five years. Why do you need a degree?"

Because the game was changing. Because credentials matter when you're trying to do the work you want to do. Because adaptation sometimes means going backward to go forward.

I finished the BS in 2024. Started the Master's in AI/ML immediately after. Finished it in 2025, at 48 years old.

Here's what nobody tells you about getting degrees later in life: it's easier in some ways. You know why you're learning. You can connect theory to practice instantly. When professors talk about overfitting or gradient descent, you've seen these problems in production. The education isn't abstract—it's validation and formalization of things you've learned through experience.

But it's also humbling. You're in classes with 22-year-olds who've never built anything real but can derive backpropagation on a whiteboard faster than you can. You learn to value different types of knowledge.

3.4 Wave 4: Using AI to Build AI (2020s)

3.4.1 The First Moment

The first time I used GPT-3 for real work, I was writing unit tests. Testing is tedious—you write the same patterns over and over, testing edge cases, mocking dependencies, asserting outcomes.

I gave GPT-3 my function signature and asked it to generate test cases.

It did. Perfectly. In seconds.

I stared at the screen. This wasn't just autocomplete. This was understanding what tests should exist for a given function. Understanding edge cases. Understanding mocking patterns.

This felt different than previous waves.

3.4.2 The Education at Evolv

At Evolv AI from 2022 to 2024, I was building generative AI systems for code generation and experimentation platforms. We needed agents that could understand code, modify it, test it, deploy it. I worked with the existing frameworks—LangChain,[20] various agentic patterns—and

---

[20] Chase, *LangChain: Building Applications with LLMs Through Composability*, 2023.

saw what worked in production and what broke.

LangChain was powerful for prototyping but fragile at scale. The imperative approach—writing agent logic as code—made workflows hard to understand, harder to modify, impossible to A/B test without full redeployments. Every behavior change required a code deployment. Every experiment meant branching code paths.

I kept thinking: there has to be a better way.

What if agents weren't written as code? What if they were described declaratively, like data? What if you could swap agent strategies by changing configuration instead of deploying code?

I sketched ideas. Built prototypes. Learned what patterns mattered—tool orchestration, conditional execution, pipeline composition. Figured out where the existing frameworks fell short.

But I didn't have the mandate or the resources to build what I was envisioning. Evolv had different priorities. So I took notes. I learned. I waited for the right opportunity.

That opportunity came when I returned to my previous employer.

3.4.3   The Return

In January 2025, I rejoined the company. Different organization than in 2019. Now they were ready for AI. Not just ML models—agentic AI systems that could understand business logic, orchestrate multiple services, make decisions in real-time.

Here's the irony: I'd left because I needed credentials to work in ML. I came back with credentials (BS, MS in AI/ML, AWS ML certification, patents). But what made me valuable wasn't the credentials.

It was that I was one of the few people who'd actually built agentic AI systems in production.

While the ML teams had deep expertise in traditional machine learning—recommendation systems, fraud detection, classification models—they hadn't built LLM orchestration systems. They hadn't deployed agents using LangChain or similar frameworks at scale. They hadn't wrestled with prompt engineering, tool selection, context management, all the messy details of production agentic AI.

I had. At Evolv, I'd built the systems, seen what broke, learned what worked. I'd already made the mistakes and figured out the solutions.

So I was given a mandate: bootstrap our agentic AI capabilities from zero.

3.4.4 Building the Foundation

Within months of returning, I had my opportunity.

The organization needed agentic AI capabilities. They had ML expertise but not LLM orchestration experience. They needed someone who'd already made the mistakes, who knew what worked in production.

I had the mandate and the resources. More importantly, I had two years of learning from Evolv about what NOT to do.

I built what I'd been envisioning:

A declarative agent framework: A language for defining agent workflows that I later formalized in an academic paper.[21] Not Python code calling LangChain—a domain-specific language that compiled to language-agnostic JSON. The same pipeline definition could execute in Java, Python, Go. You described WHAT the agent should do, not HOW to implement it.

This was ambitious. Design a language with formal grammar and semantics. Build a parser, compiler, execution engine. Support tools, LLMs, conditional execution, loops, error handling. Make it work at enterprise scale—millions of transactions, sub-100ms latency, enterprise security.

Before AI tools, this would've taken a team six months. Maybe a year.

I used AI to build AI.

Not to write everything—I designed the language semantics, the architecture, the agent primitives. Those required deep thinking about what abstractions matter, what patterns emerge in agent workflows,

---

[21] Daunis, *A Declarative Language for Building and Orchestrating LLM-Powered Agent Workflows*, 2025.

how to balance expressiveness with safety.

But AI handled the tedious implementation. Generating parsers. Writing boilerplate. Creating test cases. Implementing standard patterns. Work that would've taken weeks happened in days.

The framework gained broad adoption for deploying AI agents. It demonstrated how to integrate modern AI tooling (LangChain, Model Context Protocol) with enterprise Java systems. A companion monitoring tool provided the observability needed for production operations.

I started working on an academic paper. This wasn't just engineering— it was research. Pushing boundaries. Contributing to the academic literature on agent systems.

Combined with my earlier patent work on AI-powered biosensor systems,[22] this represented a shift in my career: from building production systems to contributing intellectual property and research.

Here's what this proved: AI doesn't replace the hard thinking. It accelerates implementation once you know what to build. The creative work—designing a language, choosing abstractions, making architectural decisions—that's entirely human.

But the tedious work of implementing those decisions? That's automatable now. And that changes everything.

I used AI to build better AI infrastructure. The pattern had come full circle.

3.4.5   The Paper

The same November 2025, I wrote an academic paper:[23] "A Declarative Language for Building and Orchestrating LLM-Powered Agent Workflows."

Fourteen pages of formal semantics, architecture diagrams, perfor-

---

[22] Daunis Llobet et al., *System and Method for Personalized Women's Health Management Using Smart Earrings AI and Mobile Application*, 2024; Daunis Llobet et al., *Wearable Devices Using Machine Learned Models for Individual-Specific Biometric Tracking and Outcome Predictions*, 2024.

[23] Daunis, *A Declarative Language for Building and Orchestrating LLM-Powered Agent Workflows*, 2025.

mance benchmarks. Real evaluation on production e-commerce workflows processing millions of interactions. Demonstrated 67% reduction in development time, 76% faster modifications, 30% fewer steps to task completion.

This wasn't just engineering—it was research. Pushing the boundaries of how we think about agent systems. Proposing new abstractions, proving they work in production, contributing to the academic literature.

The kid from Barcelona who started by learning Clipper to build accounting software was now publishing formal computer science research while leading AI development at a Fortune 500 company.

The pattern of adaptation had taken me further than I'd imagined.

3.5   The Meta-Pattern

3.5.1   The Constant in the Chaos

Looking back across twenty-five years and four major waves of "obsolescence," a clear pattern emerges.

Each wave felt existential at the time. Web editors that would replace hand-coding. Cloud platforms that would eliminate sysadmins. Libraries and frameworks that would commoditize programming. AI that would replace software engineers.

Each wave *did* automate specific tasks. Hand-coding HTML became obsolete. Manual server configuration vanished. Writing algorithms from scratch became unnecessary for most problems.

But the work didn't disappear. It transformed.

When tools automated implementation, the valuable work became architecture. When frameworks automated boilerplate, the valuable work became system design. When AI automated code generation, the valuable work became knowing what to build and why.

Here's the meta-pattern: **Automation doesn't eliminate human value. It raises the abstraction level of valuable work.**

The human computers didn't become obsolete when ENIAC arrived. They moved from calculating trajectories to programming the calculations. Same domain, higher abstraction.

I haven't become obsolete through four waves of automation. I moved from writing HTML to building frameworks to architecting systems to defining agent languages. Same industry, higher abstraction.

3.5.2 Why Some People Fail

Not everyone makes the transition successfully. Some human computers never learned programming. Some sysadmins never learned cloud architecture. Some engineers are struggling with AI tools right now.

What determines success?

It's not intelligence. Some brilliant engineers resist change. It's not experience—I've seen junior developers embrace AI faster than senior architects.

It's mindset. Specifically, it's how you answer this question: *Is my value in what I do, or in what I know how to figure out?*

If you define your value by specific skills—"I'm an expert in Puppet configuration" or "I hand-code all my algorithms"—automation is an existential threat. Your expertise has a half-life, and it's shrinking.

But if you define your value by problem-solving ability—"I can learn what I need to solve hard problems"—automation is a tool. Your expertise is learning itself, and that never becomes obsolete.

I learned this at fifteen with Clipper. I could've insisted on using C++ because that's what I knew. Instead, I learned Clipper in weeks because that's what solved the problem.

That lesson has repeated hundreds of times since. Learn Docker even though you just mastered Puppet. Learn React even though you're comfortable with jQuery. Learn prompt engineering even though you're an expert programmer.

The skill isn't expertise in any specific technology. The skill is adapting to whatever technology solves today's problems.

3.5.3 The Credential Paradox

Here's something uncomfortable: sometimes adaptation requires going backward.

I had twenty years of engineering experience when I started my Bachelor's degree at 46. I'd built systems handling millions of users. I'd filed patents. I'd led teams.

Getting a BS felt like going backward. Sitting in classes learning theory I'd already applied in practice. Writing papers about concepts I'd been using for decades.

But it wasn't backward—it was repositioning. The credential gap was keeping me from the work I wanted to do. So I fixed it.

Two years for the BS while working full-time. Another year for the MS. Three years of my late 40s spent in school.

Worth it? Absolutely. Not because the education made me better at my job—I already knew most of the material. But because the credentials opened doors. Because formal training gave me vocabulary to discuss ideas with academics and researchers. Because the process forced me to engage with theory in ways I'd avoided.

Sometimes adaptation means building bridges to where you want to go, even if the immediate path seems indirect.

3.5.4 The Age Question

People ask: "Is it too late for me to adapt?"

I got my BS at 46—the same year I started leading agentic AI work. MS at 48.

I'd been fascinated by AI since childhood—but fascination isn't expertise. Turning that interest into professional capability, formal credentials, and leadership happened in my mid-forties. Not because I couldn't have done it earlier, but because I finally committed to it.

Is it too late? Only if you think it is.

Here's what age gives you: pattern recognition. When GPT-3 arrived, I didn't panic because I'd seen this movie before. I'd seen

WYSIWYG editors, cloud platforms, frameworks, libraries. Each time, the pattern was the same: tools automate tasks, humans move up the stack.

Younger engineers might learn AI tools faster. They have fewer ingrained habits, less resistance to change. But they also lack context. They haven't seen enough cycles to recognize the pattern.

I have. That's the advantage of being older. Not faster learning, but better pattern matching. Knowing which changes matter and which are hype. Understanding where to invest time because you've seen what actually creates lasting value.

Age is only a disadvantage if you stop learning. If you keep adapting, age becomes an asset.

3.6   What This Means for You

3.6.1   The Pattern, Lived

After twenty-six years and four waves of supposed obsolescence, I've seen the Adaptation Pattern play out personally—not as theory, but as lived experience.

The Power Principle proved true every time. Every wave of technology exceeded my initial expectations. AWS became more transformative than I imagined. Docker reshaped infrastructure faster than anyone predicted. AI capabilities have grown exponentially. I learned to never bet against the technology.

The Transformation Principle saved my career. Each time a wave threatened to make my skills obsolete, new opportunities emerged at a higher level of abstraction. From writing code to designing systems. From designing systems to architecting platforms. From architecting platforms to orchestrating AI agents. The work evolved; it never disappeared.

The Early Mover Principle compounded over decades. Starting with AWS in 2007, with Docker in 2014, with LLMs in 2020—each early adoption gave me years of advantage. By the time others recognized the wave, I was already surfing the next one.

The Messy Middle Principle was real and painful. Not every transition was smooth. The 2008 financial crisis nearly killed my company. Some pivots failed. Some bets were wrong. But the overall direction held: adapt and move forward.

The Human Core Principle defined my value. What made me valuable was never execution speed. It was judgment about what to build, creativity in how to solve problems, relationships that enabled collaboration, and the ability to learn whatever came next.

3.6.2 The Practical Path

If you're facing automation anxiety right now—whether from AI or whatever comes next—here's how to apply the Adaptation Pattern:

Start using the tools immediately (Early Mover Principle). Don't wait for perfect understanding. I started using S3 when it was new and unproven. Started using GPT-3 when it was just a demo. Early adoption gives you pattern recognition before the rush.

Focus on problems, not implementations (Transformation Principle). I resisted libraries because I wanted to implement everything myself. That was ego. What matters is solving problems, not proving you can code algorithms from scratch. Let the work transform.

Build credentials before you need them (Early Mover Principle). I got my degrees while I still had a job, before I *needed* them. Don't wait until you're unemployed to retrain. Build bridges while you're still on solid ground.

Accept the mess (Messy Middle Principle). Move where the energy is. Follow the problems worth solving. Go where the interesting work is happening, even if it means leaving comfortable positions. The transition won't be clean.

Develop your human core (Human Core Principle). Share what you learn. Write papers. File patents. Give talks. Build judgment through experience. Cultivate creativity. Invest in relationships. These are the skills that never depreciate.

3.6.3   What I'm Doing Now

Right now, I'm using AI to build better AI systems. The declarative language, the agent framework, the orchestration patterns—all built with AI assistance, all designed to make AI more useful.

This is the pattern at its purest: use the new tool to build better versions of the new tool. Don't compete with AI on implementation speed. Use AI to amplify what humans do best—creative system design, architectural decisions, choosing the right abstractions.

I'm also writing this book. Sharing the pattern so others can recognize it. Because the anxiety people feel about AI is real, but it's based on incomplete information. They're living through their first automation wave. I've lived through four.

3.7   The Human Advantage Remains

Here's what AI can't do, and what I bet it won't do for a long time:

AI can't decide what's worth building. It can implement solutions once you define problems, but it can't look at a business and say "here's the problem that actually matters."

AI can't navigate organizational politics. It can't build trust with executives, can't sense which ideas will get buy-in, can't read the room in a design review.

AI can't have epiphanies. It finds patterns in existing data. It can't create genuinely novel approaches that don't exist in its training data. The declarative agent language didn't exist in GPT-4's training. AI helped me implement it, but couldn't have conceived it.

AI can't care. It optimizes metrics you give it, but it doesn't have stake in outcomes. When systems fail at 3 AM, humans fix them because we care about users, reputation, responsibility. AI doesn't have that motivation.

These limitations aren't bugs. They're the definition of where human value remains.

As we saw in Chapter 1, trust ultimately traces back to human judgment and accountability, even when machines are technically superior. That's still true today.

3.8   The Pattern Continues

I don't know what Wave 5 will be. Maybe it's AGI. Maybe it's quantum computing. Maybe it's something we can't imagine yet.

But I know the pattern will repeat. New tools will automate current work. People will panic. Some will adapt. Those who adapt will thrive.

I'll be 48 when this book publishes. I've lived through four waves already. I expect to live through several more.

Each time, I'll do what I did with Clipper at fifteen, with AWS in 2007, with Docker in 2014, with AI in 2023: learn the new tool, understand what it makes possible, build something that wasn't possible before.

The skill isn't predicting the future. It's adapting to whatever future arrives.

That's the human computer story. That's my story. That's the story of everyone who's thrived through technological change.

The only question is: will it be your story too?

The next wave is already forming. The early adopters are already learning. The opportunities are already emerging.

The pattern is reliable. Are you ready to recognize it?

Part II takes you inside the machine. I'll show you what AI agents actually do, where they fail, and why—despite the hype—companies still need you. Not theory. What I see every day building these systems.

Chapter 4

Why Companies Still Need You

4.1   The Spending Paradox

Bill Gates said it plainly: "In the future, humans won't be needed for most things."[24]

Bold statement from someone who's been right about technology trends before. And it's being quoted everywhere as evidence that AI will eliminate jobs at scale.

Meanwhile, here's what's actually happening with money:

$235 billion spent globally on AI in 2024. $1.5 trillion forecast for 2025. Big Tech alone planning $325-380 billion in capital expenditures this year. Companies are buying GPUs like they're going out of style, hiring ML teams, building AI labs, investing in infrastructure.

And what are they getting for all that spending?

According to MIT, 95% of organizations are getting zero return on their AI investments.[25] Literally zero. Not "less than expected." Not "slower than hoped." Zero.

Goldman Sachs reports that aggregate labor market impacts from AI remain "still negligible."[26] Task-level productivity gains of 10-55% show up in controlled studies, but AI's actual impact on economy-wide productivity growth is estimated at just 0.01 percentage points in 2025.

Let me put that in perspective: to justify current investments, AI

---

[24] Gates, *Bill Gates on AI: Humans Won't Be Needed 'For Most Things'*, 2025.

[25] MIT Sloan Management Review, "AI Investment Returns: Industry Survey", 2024.

[26] Goldman Sachs Research, *The Economic Impact of Artificial Intelligence*, 2024.

companies would need to generate $40 billion in annual revenue. They're currently producing $15-20 billion. That's not a small gap. That's a chasm.

And it's getting wider: 42% of companies abandoned most of their AI initiatives in 2025, up from 17% in 2024.[27]

This is starting to look like a bubble, right? Massive investment, unclear returns, lots of abandoned projects. Classic signs of hype outpacing reality.

4.2   The Silicon Valley Exception

Here's what makes my perspective different: I'm not in the 95% getting zero return.

I'm in Silicon Valley, working in production AI, seeing real production wins and actual revenue impact. Not demos. Not prototypes. Production systems handling millions of interactions, generating measurable business value, showing up in income statements.

This isn't luck. It's not that we have magic AI that works better than everyone else's. It's that we're approaching the problem differently than the companies getting zero return.

And understanding that difference is the key to understanding where human value remains—and where it's growing.

4.3   Why Most Companies Fail With AI

Let me tell you why 95% of companies are getting zero return while we're getting real results.

They're buying capability and hoping it turns into value. We're building systems that create value and using AI as one component.

That sounds subtle. It's actually fundamental.

---

[27] WorkOS, *AI Initiative Abandonment Rates in Enterprise*, 2025.

4.3.1 The Four Problems Nobody Talks About

Most AI discussions focus on what the models can do. "GPT-4 can write code! Claude can analyze data! AI will automate everything!"

But companies don't fail because the models aren't capable. They fail because of four problems that have nothing to do with model capability:

The Integration Problem. AI is good at tasks, not workflows.

The Judgment Problem. AI generates options, humans must choose.

The Trust Problem. Customers need humans for things that matter.

The Creativity Problem. Innovation requires breaking patterns, not following them.

Let me walk through each, using real examples from building AI systems in production.

4.4 The Integration Problem: Tasks vs Workflows

AI can generate code. It can analyze data. It can even provide you with an agentic workflow.

But it can't give you the workflow that actually works—that meets all business needs, keeps all constraints in mind, and integrates with your existing systems. There's engineering and data science work that a person has to do.

Here's a concrete example.

We're building an AI agent that helps users shop. Simple enough, right? AI should be able to handle this. Product search, recommendations, checkout. Standard e-commerce workflow.

Except:

- The agent needs to query our product catalog, which uses a proprietary API that's documented but complex.

- It needs to check inventory across multiple fulfillment centers with different availability rules.

- It needs to apply promotions that have Byzantine eligibility logic accumulated over years of marketing campaigns.

- It needs to handle payment through systems that have compliance requirements and fraud detection rules.

- It needs to coordinate with partner merchants who have their own APIs, data formats, and business rules.

- It needs to maintain conversation context across multiple sessions while respecting data privacy requirements.

- It needs to degrade gracefully when services are slow or unavailable without breaking the user experience.

An LLM can't just "figure this out." You can't prompt your way to understanding fifteen years of architectural decisions, partner agreements, compliance requirements, and operational constraints.

Someone needs to build the framework that lets the AI work within these constraints. Someone needs to connect service A to service B to service C. Someone needs to handle errors, manage state, ensure security, monitor performance.

That someone is a human engineer.

And here's the critical part: this isn't a temporary problem that better AI will solve. It's architectural. As long as you have complex systems built by different teams over many years, you need humans who understand those systems to orchestrate AI within them.

The declarative agent framework I built exists precisely because of this gap. AI can't build the orchestration layer. It can help implement it once you've designed it, but designing it requires understanding business requirements, technical constraints, and organizational realities that aren't in any training data.

4.4.1 The Documentation Problem

Even when APIs are well documented, documentation doesn't capture everything.

Why does this service have a 30-second timeout? Because in 2018 there was an incident where longer timeouts caused cascading failures. That's not in the API docs.

Why do we always call service X before service Y? Because Y depends on state that X creates, and that dependency isn't explicit in the interface. You just know this if you've worked on the system.

Why is this field optional in the schema but always required in practice? Because a legacy system downstream breaks without it. We've been meaning to fix it for three years.

This is tribal knowledge. It lives in people's heads, gets transmitted through code reviews and architecture discussions, accumulates through experience.

AI doesn't have access to it. And even if you fed AI every Slack message and design doc, it wouldn't have the context to know what matters and what's obsolete.

Humans provide that context. Not because we're smarter than AI at processing information, but because we lived through the decisions, understand why they were made, and know when they still apply versus when they're technical debt we're living with.

4.4.2 The "It Works, Don't Touch It" Problem

This happens constantly: instead of refactoring legacy systems, we keep maintaining them. Sometimes it's better not to touch things that work, especially if they're delicate.

There's a service that processes critical transactions. It's written in code nobody fully understands anymore. The original engineers left years ago. The documentation is incomplete. But it works. It's reliable. It handles millions of transactions.

Could AI modernize it? Technically, maybe. Generate new code that does the same thing with modern patterns.

But would you deploy that? Would you replace a battle-tested system with AI-generated code that passes tests but hasn't been proven under load, under edge cases, under the chaos of production?

No. Because when things break at scale, "the AI generated it" isn't acceptable to customers who can't complete transactions.

Humans make the judgment call: leave it alone, or refactor with extreme care. AI can help with implementation if you choose to refactor, but making that decision requires understanding risk, business impact, and organizational capacity in ways that AI can't.

4.5   The Judgment Problem: Choosing vs Generating

Ask AI to optimize a block of code for you. It suggests five approaches. Highly recommends options 1 or 2 based on common optimization patterns.

You pick number 3.

Why? Because it's easier to maintain and understand. Because it doesn't require additional memory allocation that could cause issues in constrained environments. Because the performance improvement suggested is negligible and might not even be faster when this code runs in a different system context.

AI generated the options. You made the judgment call based on context AI doesn't have.

This happens constantly. AI is great at generating possibilities. Humans are necessary for choosing among them based on factors that aren't in the optimization function.

4.5.1   The Context Problem, Again

Remember the IntelliJ example from the last chapter? AI leading you down a rabbit hole because it didn't know your Java version configuration?

That same pattern applies to every optimization, every architecture decision, every implementation choice.

AI suggests the technically optimal solution based on the code it sees. But you know:

- This team has to maintain this code, and they're more familiar with pattern X than pattern Y.

- This system is being deprecated in six months, so we're minimizing changes.

- This approach would require changes to three other services, and we don't have time for that coordination right now.

- This optimization matters on the critical path but not in background jobs where this code actually runs.

These are judgment calls. They require understanding the broader context of what you're building, why you're building it, who will maintain it, and what constraints you're operating under.

AI optimizes code. Humans optimize for business outcomes within organizational constraints. Those are different optimization problems.

4.5.2 Fine-Tuning Agentic Pipelines

This happens all the time when designing agentic pipelines. We have to fine-tune the prompt engineering, adjust the tools available, modify the workflow based on how users actually interact with the system.

A declarative framework helps with this. AI can suggest pipeline structures, but humans need to iterate on them based on business feedback, user behavior, and production metrics.

Example: A commerce agent I worked on was generating perfectly accurate product recommendations but users weren't engaging with them. Why? Because the agent was optimizing for relevance when users cared more about discovery—they wanted to be surprised, not just shown the most predictable matches.

AI can't figure that out from usage logs alone. It takes human judgment to recognize that the problem isn't accuracy, it's understanding what users actually want from the interaction.

We adjusted the pipeline to include more exploratory recommendations. User engagement improved. That required human insight about user psychology and business goals, not better AI optimization.

4.6 The Trust Problem: When It Matters, Humans Matter

Here's something I see constantly: when it's about things that matter, humans need real empathy.

Customer support is the obvious example. AI can handle routine questions—password resets, tracking information, return policies. And it does that well enough that it's worth deploying.

But when something goes wrong with a transaction? When money is involved? When someone's frustrated and needs help?

Users want humans. Not because AI can't generate appropriate responses. But because humans provide emotional validation that AI can't.

"I understand this is frustrating" means something different coming from a human who actually understands frustration versus an AI generating empathetic-sounding text.

4.6.1 The Industry Is Making Baby Steps

We can see this pattern in customer support systems across the industry. AI is handling more volume, but we're making small, careful steps. Why? Because the value is there—AI genuinely helps with routine cases—but the risk is real too.

One bad AI interaction that escalates a simple problem into an angry customer costs more than the efficiency gains from a hundred successful AI interactions.

So we deploy carefully. We keep humans in the loop for high-stakes decisions. We monitor closely. We're ready to pull back if things go wrong.

This isn't temporary caution that will disappear as AI improves. This is recognizing that trust is fragile, customers know the difference between human empathy and simulated empathy, and some interactions genuinely need the accountability that only humans provide.

4.6.2 Governance and Compliance

Then there's regulation. We want to govern ourselves. We need human oversight not just because AI makes mistakes, but because we're accountable for its decisions.

At any organization, there are parts of the system where humans must remain in the loop for trust, compliance, and legal reasons. This will remain true because of the nature of these services.

We use AI to be more productive, to be more creative, to handle more volume. But we don't rely on AI for decisions where accountability matters.

When something goes wrong with a transaction, when fraud is detected, when regulatory compliance is at stake—humans make the final calls. Not because we're better at detecting patterns (AI often is), but because someone needs to be accountable for the decision.

AI can recommend actions. Humans approve them. That separation matters legally, ethically, and practically.

4.7 The Creativity Problem: Breaking Patterns

AI finds patterns in data. Innovation requires breaking patterns.

Let me give you a concrete example from my own work: the Incora Earring project, where I'm one of the co-inventors with two provisional patents.[28][29]

---

[28] Daunis Llobet et al., *System and Method for Personalized Women's Health Management Using Smart Earrings AI and Mobile Application*, 2024.

[29] Daunis Llobet et al., *Wearable Devices Using Machine Learned Models for Individual-Specific Biometric Tracking and Outcome Predictions*, 2024.

The insight was simple: there was no product that would actually measure core body temperature accurately and that you could comfortably wear at night. Smartwatches are uncomfortable for sleeping. Chest straps are awkward. Rings measure peripheral temperature, not core.

But earrings? Women already wear them. They're positioned near major blood vessels. They're socially acceptable for continuous wear. The form factor solves multiple problems simultaneously.

Could AI have suggested this?

No. Because it required combining insights from multiple domains that don't appear together in training data:

- Women's health monitoring needs

- Wearable technology constraints

- Biosensor capabilities positioned at different body locations

- Social acceptability patterns for different wearable form factors

- Sleep comfort considerations

This is creative synthesis. Seeing a solution by combining knowledge from disparate domains in ways that create something genuinely novel.

AI can help implement the solution once you've conceived it. It can optimize sensor placement, suggest algorithms for temperature analysis, generate code for data processing. But conceiving the approach in the first place? That required human creativity.

4.7.1 The Market Opportunity Question

Another example: identifying market opportunities that AI wouldn't predict.

When I started building the declarative agent framework, there was no market demand for it. LangChain existed. Companies were using it. Nobody was explicitly asking for a declarative alternative.

I built it because I saw a problem that would emerge: as companies moved agents from prototypes to production, the imperative approach would become unmaintainable. But that wasn't obvious from market signals. It required extrapolating from experience with other technologies.

AI looks at current patterns. Humans anticipate future needs based on understanding how technologies evolve, how organizations adopt them, and what problems emerge at scale.

That's not pattern matching. It's pattern projection—imagining how current trends will create future problems that don't exist yet.

4.8 The Real Economic Equation

So why do companies still need humans? Not for tasks. Tasks are increasingly automatable.

Companies need humans who multiply AI's effectiveness.

4.8.1 The Engineers Who Build Infrastructure

That's what I do. I don't compete with AI on writing code. I build the infrastructure that lets AI work at enterprise scale—the frameworks, the orchestration systems, the integration layers.

This role is more valuable now than before AI, not less. Because the gap between "AI can do this in a demo" and "AI can do this in production at scale" is enormous, and bridging that gap requires engineering expertise.

4.8.2 The Product Managers Who Know When

Product managers who understand when to use AI and when not to. When automation improves user experience and when it degrades it. When AI can handle a workflow and when humans need to remain involved.

This judgment is valuable precisely because AI can't make it. Someone needs to understand users well enough to know what they want automated and what they want human.

4.8.3 The Leaders Who Orchestrate

Leaders who can orchestrate teams of humans plus AI tools to solve complex problems. Who understand what work to assign to AI, what work requires human judgment, and how to design workflows that leverage both effectively.

This is a skill that didn't exist five years ago and is now critical. It's not being AI-savvy or being a good manager. It's being both simultaneously and understanding how to multiply their effects.

4.9 The Shift In What Companies Want

Here's something concrete I'm seeing: the skills companies want have fundamentally changed in the last five years.

Five years ago, when I wanted to work in ML roles and lacked credentials, companies wanted data scientists with PhDs. Deep expertise in statistics, machine learning theory, research methodology. The assumption was that ML was a research problem—you needed people who could develop novel algorithms, understand mathematical foundations, publish papers.

Now? Companies want engineers who can build AI infrastructure.

Why the shift? Because AI-as-infrastructure requires engineering skills more than research skills.

You don't need to develop novel algorithms—you use pre-trained models. You don't need to prove mathematical theorems—you need to deploy systems at scale. You don't need to write papers—you need to write production code that handles millions of requests reliably.

The valuable skill isn't understanding how transformers work mathematically. It's understanding how to integrate LLMs into production systems, how to handle errors gracefully, how to optimize for latency and cost, how to build frameworks that other engineers can use.

4.9.1 How My Hiring Criteria Changed

Two years ago, I looked for candidates with traditional ML and Big Data software engineering experience. Spark, Hadoop, scikit-learn. People who could build data pipelines and train models.

This year, every candidate I interviewed, I looked for either experience in LLMs, Agentic AI, or MLOps. And every candidate had used AI tools for code generation at their previous work.

That's not a coincidence. It's the market recognizing what matters now.

The demand is massive. Companies are competing for people who can actually build with AI, not just talk about it. Who understand both the domain—payments, commerce, whatever the business is—and AI capabilities.

That combination is rare and valuable.

4.9.2 The Ironic Reversal

Here's what's ironic: five years ago, companies were trying to move from software engineers to data scientists. "We need more people with stats PhDs! More ML researchers! More people who understand the math!"

Now they're moving back to software engineers. But not the same software engineers—engineers who understand AI infrastructure, who've built with LLMs, who know how to deploy agentic systems.

It's a pendulum swing, but at a higher level of abstraction. We're not going back to where we were. We're going forward to a place where engineering skills matter more than research skills, but the engineering has become more sophisticated.

4.10 What About Tech Layoffs?

Let me address the elephant in the room: tech companies have been laying people off. Meta, Google, Amazon, Microsoft. Tens of thousands of jobs eliminated.

Is this AI replacing humans?

No. This is normal business cycles.

Major tech companies have turnover rates of 10-20%. Some of that is voluntary—people leaving for other opportunities. Some is involuntary—performance management, reorganizations, business priorities shifting.

The 2024-2025 layoffs are large, but they're happening because companies over-hired during the pandemic boom and are now correcting. They're driven by economic conditions, interest rates, advertising revenue, profitability targets.

Not by AI capability suddenly making humans obsolete.

Here's how you know: if AI were replacing humans, you'd see different patterns. You'd see specific roles disappearing—data entry, customer support, junior developers. You'd see hiring freezes for those roles while other roles continue hiring.

Instead, you see broad cuts across departments. Finance and engineering and sales. Entry level and senior. Research and implementation. That's not "AI is replacing role X." That's "we need to cut costs across the board."

Companies are blaming AI because it sounds better than "we over-hired and now we're correcting." But the actual driver is business cycles, not technological replacement.

4.10.1 Jobs Are Transforming, Not Disappearing

What I am seeing: roles changing, not vanishing.

"ML Engineer" is becoming "AI Engineer." The work is different—less about training models from scratch, more about deploying and orchestrating pre-trained models. But it's not fewer jobs. If anything, there's more demand because more companies need this capability.

"Data Scientist" is increasingly overlapping with "Software Engineer." You need to know statistics, but you also need to build production systems. The pure researcher role that only develops models without deploying them is becoming rare.

New specializations are emerging: prompt engineers, agent designers,

MLOps specialists, AI infrastructure engineers. Roles that didn't exist two years ago and now have significant demand.

Same team sizes, different skills. We're not cutting headcount because AI does the work. We're shifting what work people do toward the things AI can't handle—orchestration, judgment, creativity, accountability.

4.11 The 5% vs The 95%

So back to the spending paradox: why are 95% of companies getting zero return while we're getting measurable value?

Because they're trying to replace humans with AI. We're trying to augment humans with AI.

They're buying capability and hoping it turns into value. We're identifying where human judgment matters and using AI to multiply it.

They're deploying AI and discovering integration problems, judgment gaps, trust issues, creativity limitations. We're designing around those limitations from the start.

They're treating AI as a replacement for people. We're treating it as a tool that makes people more effective.

That difference determines whether you get zero return or measurable business value.

4.12 What This Means For You

If you're worried about AI eliminating your job, you're asking the wrong question.

The right question: are you multiplying AI's effectiveness, or competing with it?

If you're trying to be faster at tasks than AI, you'll lose. AI will keep getting faster, cheaper, more capable at task-level work.

If you're providing judgment, orchestration, creativity, and accountability that AI can't provide, you're becoming more valuable as AI improves.

The economic reality isn't "humans vs AI." It's "humans who use AI vs humans who don't."

Companies aren't eliminating engineers. They're eliminating engineers who can't or won't work with AI tools. They're competing to hire engineers who can build AI infrastructure, orchestrate AI systems, and provide the judgment that makes AI useful instead of just impressive.

That's the actual economic equation. Not replacement. Augmentation.

And the opportunity is massive. Not despite AI, but because of it. Because the gap between AI capability and AI value is enormous, and bridging that gap requires exactly the skills that humans provide.

But to understand exactly where human value lies, you first need to see what AI agents actually do—from the inside. Not the hype. Not the fear. The reality of what I build every day.

And that's what comes next.

Chapter 5

What AI Agents Can Actually Do

5.1 The Irony Isn't Lost on Me

I build the systems everyone fears.

Every day, I work on AI agents that automate tasks software engineers used to do manually. Code generation. System orchestration. Data analysis. Decision-making workflows. The exact kinds of capabilities that make people wonder if their jobs are safe.

And I'm not theorizing about this. I'm not a consultant writing slide decks about AI's potential. I'm writing the code, deploying the systems, watching them handle millions of interactions in production. I see what works and what breaks. I understand both the impressive capabilities and the embarrassing failures.

Here's what makes my perspective different: I'm building these systems while simultaneously betting my own career on understanding them correctly. If I'm wrong about where human value remains, I'm automating myself into irrelevance. If I'm right, I'm building tools that make human engineers more valuable, not less.

The stakes are personal. And after a year of building agentic AI infrastructure from the ground up, I have strong opinions about what's real and what's hype.

5.2 What "Agentic" Actually Means

Let me cut through the buzzwords and explain what we're actually building.

5.2.1 Three Levels of AI Systems

Think of AI capabilities as existing on three levels:

Level 1: Traditional APIs. This is how user interfaces communicate with applications. You click a button, it sends a request to a server, the server runs predetermined logic, returns a result. Everything is explicit. The computer does exactly what you programmed it to do, nothing more.

Example: You click "Add to Cart" on a product page. The API receives your product ID, checks inventory, updates your cart database, returns a confirmation. Simple, deterministic, completely predictable.

Level 2: LLM-Powered Systems. Think of this as a super-powered autocomplete system. It's using a massive database of human knowledge—all the text humanity has written, compressed into mathematical representations—combined with reinforcement learning to predict what comes next.

Example: You type "How do I reset my password?" and the system generates a helpful response based on patterns it learned from millions of similar conversations. It's not following a script. It's predicting what a helpful human would say.

This is impressive but limited. The LLM can only generate responses. It can't actually reset your password, check your account status, or take any action beyond producing text.

Level 3: Agentic AI Systems. This is where it gets interesting. Agents can use actual tools. They can communicate with applications iteratively. They can take actions, observe results, adjust their approach, and try again.

Example: You say "I forgot my password and need to reset it." An agentic system can:

1. Verify your identity by asking security questions

2. Call the password reset API

3. Send you a verification code

4. Confirm the code you enter

5. Update your password

6. Verify you can log in with the new password

It's not just generating text about how to reset passwords. It's actually orchestrating the entire workflow, adapting to whatever responses it gets, handling errors gracefully.

That's what makes it "agentic"—the ability to pursue a goal through multiple steps, using tools, adapting to feedback, until the task is complete.

5.3   The Configuration Insight

When I rejoined PayPal in early 2025, I encountered a common pattern in enterprise AI: agents built using existing frameworks like LangChain[30] in Python, with some custom implementations in Java.

Every agent was written as code. Want to change how an agent behaves? Deploy new code. Want to A/B test two agent strategies? Deploy two versions of the application with branching logic. Want to add a new capability? Write code, test it, deploy it through the full CI/CD pipeline.

This is painful at any large organization. Not because the frameworks are bad—LangChain is powerful. But because agent behavior feels like something that should be configurable, not hard-coded.

---

[30] Chase, *LangChain: Building Applications with LLMs Through Composability*, 2023.

Here's what I realized: **Application deployments are complex. Configuration deployments are simple.**

Deploying a new version of a Java application at enterprise scale involves:

- Code reviews across multiple teams

- Security scanning and compliance checks

- Integration testing with dozens of dependent services

- Staged rollouts to prevent outages

- Rollback procedures if anything breaks

- Coordination across time zones and organizations

It takes days, sometimes weeks. That's appropriate for application code—you want those safeguards.

But deploying a configuration change?

- Update a JSON file

- Validate it against a schema

- Push to configuration service

- Agents load new config automatically

- Rollback is instant if needed

It takes minutes. Sometimes seconds.

The insight: **What if you define agents as configuration instead of code?**

That's not just a convenience. It fundamentally changes how fast you can iterate. When agent behavior is configuration data, you can:

A/B test agent strategies trivially. Deploy five different pipeline variants to the same application instance. Route 20% of traffic to each. Collect metrics automatically. Pick the winner. All without touching application code.

Let non-engineers modify agents safely. Product managers can adjust prompts, add tools, change workflows—all through configuration that gets validated before deployment. They can experiment without breaking production.

Version control agent behavior like data. Every change is a git commit. Diffs show exactly what changed. Rollbacks are instant. You can trace every agent decision back to the exact configuration that produced it.

Deploy agents across different languages. The same JSON pipeline definition executes in Java services, Python services, Go services. One specification, multiple implementations. Build it once, run it everywhere.

This is the core insight behind the declarative approach. Not just "let's build agent infrastructure." But "let's treat agents as data that describes behavior, not code that implements behavior." The difference sounds subtle. The implications are enormous.

5.4 What This Looks Like in Production

Let me give you a real example of what agentic AI does.

5.4.1 A Commerce Agent in Action

To illustrate what agentic AI looks like in practice, consider a conversational shopping assistant. Imagine you open an app and say:

"It's my wedding anniversary next week and I want to impress my partner."

Here's what happens behind the scenes:

Understanding Context. The agent knows you're shopping for your partner based on your profile and purchase history. It understands "impress" means you want something special, not just functional.

Product Search. It queries a product catalog with semantic search—not just keyword matching, but understanding intent. "Anniversary gift that impresses" maps to jewelry, experiences, luxury items.

Personalization. It filters results based on your partner's preferences (if known), your typical spending range, your past purchases. Not showing you $50,000 watches if you usually spend $200 on gifts.

Recommendation. It presents options with reasoning: "Based on your partner's interest in art, these gallery event tickets might be perfect." Not just showing products, but explaining why they're relevant.

Conversational Refinement. You say "Something more personal." It adjusts—now looking at custom items, personalized gifts, things with emotional value.

Transaction Completion. When you decide, you don't leave the conversation. "I'll take the gallery tickets." The agent adds them to your cart, applies any relevant offers, confirms your payment method, completes the purchase. All through natural language.

This entire workflow—understanding intent, searching products, personalizing results, handling conversation, completing transactions—is what a declarative agent framework enables. The agent follows a pipeline that describes what to do at each step, not imperative code that hard-codes every decision.

When you want to improve such an agent—better product selection, more personalization, smoother checkout flow—you update the pipeline configuration. Deploy in minutes. Measure results. Iterate.

Such agents handle thousands of conversations simultaneously. Each one adapting to the user's context, navigating through different paths based on responses, using tools as needed.

That's what "agentic" means in practice. Not just answering questions, but accomplishing goals through multistep workflows that adapt to feedback.

5.5 What Still Feels Like Magic

I build these systems. I understand the architecture. I know it's matrix multiplication and probability distributions all the way down.

And it still feels like magic every single time.

The accuracy of responses is what surprises me most. Not that LLMs can generate fluent text—that stopped being impressive in 2023. But that they can understand subtle context, maintain coherence across long conversations, adapt to user intent shifts, and produce responses that genuinely help people accomplish goals.

Example: A user asks about a product, mentions in passing that they're concerned about sustainability, later talks about price sensitivity. The agent remembers all three constraints and surfaces products that are eco-friendly, affordable, and relevant to the original query. It connects dots across multiple conversation turns in ways that feel genuinely intelligent.

I know how this works technically—attention mechanisms, context windows, fine-tuning on conversational data. But knowing the mechanism doesn't diminish the wonder. It's like understanding aerodynamics doesn't make flight less amazing.

What impresses me isn't the raw capability of the models. It's what becomes possible when you give them the right tools, the right context, and the right structure to operate within. The whole becomes greater than the sum of its parts.

An LLM by itself can generate text. An LLM with access to product catalogs, payment systems, user profiles, and orchestration logic? That can solve real problems for real users at scale.

That's what we're building. And every day, I see interactions that make me think "yeah, this actually works."

5.6   What Frustrates Me About the Hype

But let me be clear about what frustrates me.

5.6.1   The Job Elimination Panic

The people who think AI will eliminate all jobs. This drives me crazy.

I'm literally building the automation systems, and I see zero evidence that we're heading toward mass unemployment. What I see is work transforming. Tasks getting automated. Humans moving to higher-level problems.

The pattern I've lived through four times isn't breaking. It's accelerating.

Yes, some specific tasks will get automated. Code generation, data analysis, content creation. But those are tasks, not jobs. Jobs are bundles of tasks plus judgment, context, relationships, strategy.

AI handles tasks. Humans provide judgment about which tasks matter and why.

The panic comes from people who've never lived through an automation wave before. They look at AI automating their current tasks and assume that's the end. They don't see that new, higher-value tasks emerge when the old ones get automated.

I get it. It's scary when you see AI doing what you do. But history is consistent: automate tasks, humans move up the value chain, total employment increases, work becomes more interesting.

Betting against that pattern has been wrong every single time.

5.6.2   The AI Apocalypse Narrative

Then there's the opposite extreme: people saying AI will rule the world, make all decisions, lead to Terminator-style apocalypse.

This is just as ridiculous.

AI systems are tools. Extremely powerful tools, yes. Tools that can automate complex workflows, yes. But they're optimization engines, not autonomous agents with their own goals.

An AI doesn't "want" anything. It doesn't have ambitions. It optimizes whatever objective function you give it, within whatever constraints you set. That's it.

The risks are real, but they're boring. Not "AI becomes sentient and decides humans are the problem." More like "AI optimizes for engagement and accidentally creates addictive behavior patterns" or "AI trained on biased data perpetuates those biases at scale."

These are serious problems. But they're human problems—problems of what we choose to optimize for, what data we train on, what constraints we enforce. AI doesn't decide to be harmful. Humans make design choices that lead to harmful outcomes.

The solution isn't fearing AI. It's building AI systems with proper constraints, oversight, and alignment with human values. Which is exactly what we're doing.

5.6.3 The Guilt About Using AI

Here's what bothers me most: people who hide their use of AI or feel guilty about it.

I see this constantly. Engineers who use Copilot but don't admit it. Writers who use ChatGPT but pretend they didn't. Students who get AI help but feel like they're cheating.

This is backwards.

Using AI tools makes you more productive, not less skilled. Using a calculator doesn't make you bad at math. Using an IDE doesn't make you bad at programming. Using AI doesn't make you bad at thinking.

What makes you less skilled is refusing to learn new tools because of some misplaced sense of purity.

Here's reality: in five years, the engineers who are thriving will be those who learned to work effectively with AI tools. The engineers who refused to use them because "real programmers write everything from scratch" will be struggling.

This isn't a moral question. It's a practical one. The tools exist. They're getting better exponentially. Using them effectively is a skill you need to build.

Don't feel guilty. Feel behind if you're not using them yet.

5.7 The Junior Engineer Transformation

Here's something concrete I've seen that would've been impossible a few years ago.

We have junior engineers—fresh out of college, spent their entire education writing Python—who are now committing code to our Java services regularly.

Not just reading Java. Not just making trivial changes. Writing meaningful features, fixing complex bugs, implementing new APIs.

How? They're using AI to bridge the language gap.

They'll say "I need to implement this feature in Java" and have an AI-assisted conversation:

> Engineer: "How do I do dependency injection in Java?"
>
> AI: [Generates Spring example with explanation]
>
> Engineer: "Our service uses Guice, not Spring. Show me with Guice."
>
> AI: [Generates Guice example]
>
> Engineer: "This doesn't match our patterns. Here's how we structure services..."
>
> AI: [Adapts to their specific codebase patterns]

Then they write the code, test it, submit a pull request. Reviewers give feedback. They iterate. They learn.

A crazy thought just a few years ago: Python developers becoming productive Java contributors in weeks instead of months.

But here's the key: they're learning by doing. Not reading documentation for months before touching code. Writing code immediately, with AI filling in syntax and patterns they don't know yet. Building muscle memory through practice.

The AI isn't replacing their thinking. It's accelerating their learning loop. They still need to understand the problem, design the solution, review the code, fix bugs. But they're not blocked by not knowing Java syntax or Spring conventions.

This is what AI amplification looks like in practice. Not eliminating engineers. Helping engineers become productive in new domains faster than was previously possible.

And you know what? The code quality is often better than what you'd get from a junior engineer without AI assistance. Because the AI suggests idiomatic patterns, catches common mistakes, follows best practices.

The junior engineer still needs to review and understand the code. But they're starting from better examples than they would generate on their own.

5.8 The Trajectory: Better and Cheaper

People ask: "Is AI really improving as fast as people claim?"

Yes. Unambiguously yes.

Two metrics matter: **model capability** and **cost per token**.

5.8.1 Capability Improvements

When GPT-3 launched in 2020, it could generate impressive text but was unreliable for structured tasks. It would hallucinate confidently, lose context in long conversations, struggle with complex reasoning.

GPT-4 in 2023 was a significant leap. Reliable enough for production use. Good at maintaining context. Capable of following complex instructions.

GPT-4o, Claude 3.5 Sonnet, and the latest models? They're qualitatively better. Longer context windows. Better instruction following. More reliable tool use. Fewer hallucinations.

But the real improvement isn't any single capability. It's reliability. The models work consistently enough that you can build production systems on top of them and trust they'll behave predictably.

That's the phase transition. When reliability crosses the threshold where you can build critical business logic on top of AI, everything changes.

We're past that threshold now.

5.8.2 Cost Improvements

The cost curve is even more dramatic.

In 2020, running GPT-3 at scale was prohibitively expensive. Only large companies could afford serious production deployments.

Today? Costs have dropped by 10-100x depending on model and use case. And they're still falling.

This matters because cost determines what's economically viable to automate. When AI was expensive, you only used it for high-value tasks where automation justified the cost. As costs fall, more and more tasks become worth automating.

The implication: the scope of what AI can economically handle keeps expanding. Tasks that weren't worth automating last year are worth automating now. Tasks that aren't worth automating now will be worth automating next year.

The trajectory is clear. Models keep getting better. Costs keep falling. The range of economically viable AI applications keeps expanding.

5.9 What This Actually Means

So what do you do with this information?

If you're a software engineer, product manager, data scientist—anyone doing knowledge work—you need to understand how the Adaptation Pattern applies specifically to AI.

The Power Principle is in full effect. AI capabilities are real and improving fast. This isn't hype. The systems work in production at scale. They're not perfect, but they're good enough to build on, and they're getting exponentially better. Dismissing AI as a fad violates everything we know about technological waves. The question isn't whether AI will transform your work. It's how fast and how completely.

The Transformation Principle applies at the task level. Specific tasks you do today will get automated. That doesn't make you obsolete—it frees you to focus on higher-level problems. But only if you adapt. Only if you learn to work with AI tools rather than competing against them. The work is transforming right now. Your job is to transform with it.

The Human Core Principle defines your future value. Understanding both AI's capabilities and limitations is the skill that matters. I know what AI does well because I build it. I know what it fails at because I see the failures daily. That dual understanding—seeing both power and constraints—is what lets you use AI effectively instead of either overestimating or underestimating it.

5.10 Why I'm Telling You This

I'm in a unique position. I'm building the automation systems while simultaneously betting my career on understanding them correctly.

If AI were really going to replace engineers, I'd be the first to know. I'm writing the systems that would do the replacing.

And I'm not worried. Not because I'm special or irreplaceable. But because I see daily what AI can and can't do.

It can handle tasks. It can't provide judgment about which tasks matter.

It can implement solutions. It can't decide what problems are worth solving.

It can generate code. It can't architect systems that align with business needs and organizational constraints.

It can optimize defined objectives. It can't determine what objectives are right.

The gap between task automation and human replacement is enormous. Crossing it requires capabilities AI doesn't have and shows no signs of developing.

But here's the critical part: the humans who thrive will be those who learn to use AI tools effectively. Not those who compete with AI on AI's terms, trying to type faster or memorize more. But those who focus on what humans uniquely provide: judgment, creativity, context, relationships.

The next chapter explores exactly what AI can't do—and why those limitations define where human value remains.

Because understanding AI's capabilities is important. But understanding its limitations? That's where you find your future.

Chapter 6

Where the Machine Still Fails

6.1 The Gap Between Promise and Reality

In 2024, Humane Inc. launched the AI Pin with massive hype.[31] The pitch was seductive: a screenless, wearable device that would replace your smartphone. No more staring at screens. Just talk to your AI assistant through voice commands, see information projected onto your hand via laser, handle calls, texts, searches, translations, photos—all without pulling out your phone.

The market responded with cautious optimism. Maybe this was the next evolution of computing. Maybe we really were ready to move beyond smartphones.

It failed. Spectacularly.

Not because the technology didn't work—it mostly did. But because it failed to understand something fundamental about why smartphones succeeded in the first place. Phones aren't just hardware and features. They're ecosystems. Apps. Proven UI patterns. Twenty years of behavioral adaptation. Muscle memory. Infrastructure.

The Humane AI Pin asked people to abandon all of that for... what exactly? Voice commands that were sometimes slow? A laser projection that only worked in specific lighting? A device that cost $700 plus $24 monthly subscription to do less than the phone already in your pocket?

When I saw the demos, I knew it wouldn't work. Not because the

---
[31] Humane Inc., *Humane AI Pin Product Launch and Market Reception*, 2024.

technology was bad, but because they fundamentally misunderstood how technology adoption works.

Think about it: Google hasn't significantly changed its search interface in twenty years. Not because they can't innovate, but because that simple search box is burned into billions of people's muscle memory. Apple moves interface elements by two pixels and people complain. Microsoft changes a menu structure and enterprise customers revolt.

UI changes happen in small, iterative steps. Not revolutionary jumps.

The Humane AI Pin asked for a revolutionary jump. From screens to no screens. From touch to voice. From visual feedback to... hoping the laser works in sunlight. That's not how humans adopt technology.

6.1.1 The Next Failure: Neo the Robot Housekeeper

Now watch the same pattern repeat with 1X Technologies' Neo robot.[32]

The promise: a humanoid robot that helps around your house. Your personal housekeeper. Your "Star Trek: The Next Generation Data" that cleans, organizes, assists. The future of domestic automation.

The reality: what's shipping in 2026 is a teleoperated prototype. Humans controlling it remotely. Not autonomous AI making decisions. Not a robot that understands your preferences and adapts to your home. A expensive telepresence system with robotic hands.

This will fail for the same reason the AI Pin failed: the gap between what's promised and what's deliverable is enormous.

To succeed, Neo would need:

- Vision models with complete environmental understanding

- LLM reasoning combined with agentic AI that can plan multi-step tasks

- Advanced robotics that can handle the physical chaos of real homes

---

[32] 1X Technologies, *NEO Humanoid Robot*, 2025.

- Understanding of individual preferences and ambiguous instructions

- Ability to adapt to novel situations not in training data

We're not close to having all of these simultaneously. We might get there eventually. But selling the dream now, delivering a teleoperated toy later? That's how you poison the market for when the technology actually is ready.

6.2 Why the Hype Gap Exists

Here's what I've learned building AI systems at multiple companies: **startups lie**. Not all of them. But most do.

Some lie knowingly. They understand the technology's limitations but oversell anyway because that's how you raise money, get press, build hype. The plan is to figure out the hard parts later, after you've secured funding and mindshare.

Some lie unknowingly. The executives making promises are driven by spreadsheets and market projections, not technical reality. They genuinely believe the engineers will solve the hard problems because, in their mental model, all technical problems are solvable given enough resources.

Both approaches hurt the same people: the product and development teams who have to deliver on impossible promises.

As someone building AI systems, I feel this tension constantly. Demos are almost never real. They're carefully constructed scenarios designed to impress stakeholders. Investors don't want to hear about limitations—they want to hear about billion-dollar markets and exponential growth.

But here's the thing: over-promising and under-delivering doesn't just hurt your company. It hurts the entire field. When high-profile AI products fail to deliver, people stop trusting AI generally. Real, working AI systems get dismissed as hype. Engineers building genuine solutions face skepticism because previous companies cried wolf.

The responsible path is harder: promise less, deliver more. Show what actually works. Be honest about limitations. Build trust through reliability, not through hype.

That's what this chapter is about. Not what AI might do someday. What it fundamentally can't do, and why those limitations matter.

6.3 The Context Problem: When Reality Isn't in the Data

Let me give you a concrete example from my daily work.

You're developing in IntelliJ. Your Java project won't compile. You've spent an hour trying different things. Nothing works. So you copy the error log and paste it into your enterprise AI assistant.

The AI analyzes the error. Suggests solutions. You try them. They don't work. It suggests more solutions. You try those. Still broken. You're now two hours into this rabbit hole, following every suggestion, making configuration changes, rebuilding caches, reimporting projects.

The actual problem? Your system has both Java 17.0.8 and 17.0.14 installed. Your environment is configured for 17.0.8. Your project is trying to use 17.0.14. That's it. That's the whole problem.

The AI will never catch this. Not because it's not smart enough, but because it doesn't have the context that your environment is configured for a specific patch version. It can't intuit that you overlooked a version mismatch. It has no way to know what's installed on your machine versus what your IDE is configured to use.

So it keeps trying to help. Suggesting progressively more exotic solutions. Leading you further down the rabbit hole.

A human engineer who's seen this before would ask: "What Java version is your IDE configured for? What's actually installed?" Two questions, thirty seconds, problem solved.

This is the context problem in a nutshell: **AI can give you plausible answers based on the context it has. But it can't know what context it's missing.**

The more context AI has, the better its answers. But there's always context it doesn't have. And often, that missing context is exactly what matters.

6.3.1 Context That Lives in Heads, Not Data

At any organization, humans have knowledge that exists nowhere in documentation.

"We tried that architecture in 2019. It looked good on paper but caused cascading failures under load. Here's why..."

"That team has political constraints because of a re-org two years ago. If you want this approved, you need to route it through this VP, not that one."

"This executive cares deeply about customer trust. Any feature that could be perceived as surveillance will get killed, even if it's technically sound."

"That partner has a clause in their contract that prevents us from doing X, even though it makes technical sense."

This is organizational memory. It's not in Confluence pages or Slack archives. It's in people's heads, accumulated through experience, shared through conversations, transmitted through culture.

You could try connecting everything corporate to AI—every document, every Slack message, every meeting recording. Maybe that's the next wave. But even then, you'd miss the unspoken context. The things people know but never write down because they're "obvious" to anyone who was there.

AI sees patterns in data. Humans understand reality that includes things not in the data.

6.3.2 When I Choose Not to Automate

I still respond to Slack messages myself. Even though I could easily build an AI agent to handle routine questions.

Why? Because conversations have subtext. Someone asking "Is

this ready?" might actually be asking "I need this urgently, can you prioritize it?" or "I'm blocked, please help" or "I'm checking if you forgot about this."

The words are the same. The meaning is different. And the appropriate response depends on reading context that isn't in the message.

Could AI learn this? Maybe. With enough examples, enough training on my communication patterns, enough context about relationships and urgency signals. Maybe.

But even then: I *want* to respond myself. Because these are relationships. Because I care about helping people. Because sometimes the conversation reveals something unexpected that needs my attention.

The automation is technically possible. I choose not to do it because the human context matters more than the efficiency gain.

6.4   The Ambiguity Problem: When "Right" Isn't Enough

Here's something I see constantly: the problem people *say* they have isn't the problem they *actually* have.

Someone says: "The agent is too slow."

Real problem: Lack of progress indicators made it *feel* slow. The agent completed tasks in reasonable time, but users sitting in silence for 30 seconds assumed it was broken.

Solution: Not making it faster. Adding "I'm thinking..." and "Searching products..." and "Analyzing options..." feedback. Users need to see the machine thinking, even if the machine doesn't actually need to show its work.

Someone says: "The agent makes mistakes."

Real problem: Users couldn't tell when the agent was confident versus guessing. When it was 95% sure versus 60% sure. So every answer felt equally unreliable.

Solution: Not improving accuracy. Adding confidence indicators. Saying "Based on your preferences, I'm confident this product matches" versus "I think this might work but I'm not certain." Transparency about uncertainty.

Someone says: "The agent needs better memory."

Real problem: Users wanted selective forgetting, not total recall. They wanted the agent to remember preferences but forget embarrassing searches. Remember address for shipping but forget that 3am impulse purchase they regretted.

Solution: Not more memory. Better control over what gets remembered.

Someone says: "The agent should be proactive."

Real problem: Users found unsolicited actions creepy. They wanted agency on demand, not an AI assistant constantly suggesting things they didn't ask for.

Solution: Not more proactivity. Better framing. Let users opt-in to suggestions rather than pushing them automatically.

See the pattern? The technical solution is clear in each case. The hard part is figuring out what problem you're actually solving.

An AI optimizing for "make the agent faster" would focus on latency. It wouldn't realize that perceived speed matters more than actual speed. That users will happily wait 60 seconds if they see progress, but will abandon after 20 seconds of silence.

An AI optimizing for "reduce errors" would focus on accuracy. It wouldn't realize that confidence calibration matters more than raw correctness. That being right 80% of the time while *saying* you're 80% confident is better than being right 85% of the time while acting 100% certain.

These are judgment calls. They require understanding human psychology, not just optimizing metrics.

6.4.1   Why We Don't Let Agents Auto-Commit

We could easily let our coding agents auto-commit and push code without human review. The agents generate correct code. They pass tests. They follow style guidelines.

We don't let them do it. Even though it would be faster. Even though the code is often 100% accurate.

Why? Because at enterprise level, we don't let *humans* push code without two other people reviewing it. Not because we don't trust individual engineers, but because code review catches things beyond correctness:

- "This solves the immediate problem but creates technical debt here."

- "This pattern works but violates our architectural principles."

- "This is correct but there's a simpler approach."

- "This will work today but won't scale when traffic increases."

These aren't bugs. They're judgment calls about maintainability, scalability, consistency with team practices.

Could AI learn to make these judgments? Theoretically. With enough training on our codebase, our architectural decisions, our long-term strategy.

But here's the deeper issue: we want humans in the loop because when something breaks, someone needs to be accountable. If an AI-generated feature causes an outage, who's responsible? The AI? The person who approved deploying it? The team that trained it?

The answer: the humans who decided to let AI ship code without human review.

So we keep humans in the loop. Not because AI can't generate correct code, but because correctness isn't the only thing that matters.

6.4.2 The Cascading Failure Problem

There's another reason for human oversight: agents acting on agents creates cascading failures.

Agent A generates code. Agent B reviews it automatically. Agent C deploys it. Agent D monitors for errors. Agent E tries to fix errors automatically.

Somewhere in that chain, something goes wrong. Maybe Agent A misunderstood requirements. Maybe Agent B missed a subtle bug. Maybe Agent C deployed to the wrong environment. Maybe Agent D's error detection has a false negative. Maybe Agent E's fix makes things worse.

By the time humans notice, you have five layers of automated decisions compounding each other's mistakes.

Humans in the loop at key decision points prevent these cascades. Not because humans don't make mistakes—we do. But because we're accountable. We care about outcomes. We take responsibility when things break.

If an agent speaks for us, its mistakes are our mistakes. That's just how it works.

6.5 Innovation That Can't Be Trained

Sure, AI can help you brainstorm and generate new ideas. But let me tell you about my patents—how they came to be and why I think genuine innovation follows a different process entirely, one that can't be trained into a model.

6.5.1 The Biosensor Earrings

Two of my patents are about personalized women's health management using smart earrings with biosensors.[33][34] The earrings continuously monitor physiological signals—temperature, heart rate variability, stress markers. A mobile application uses machine learning and natural language processing to interpret this data and provide personalized health insights.

Could AI have invented this?

No. Not because the individual components are novel—biosensors

---

[33] Daunis Llobet et al., *System and Method for Personalized Women's Health Management Using Smart Earrings AI and Mobile Application*, 2024.

[34] Daunis Llobet et al., *Wearable Devices Using Machine Learned Models for Individual-Specific Biometric Tracking and Outcome Predictions*, 2024.

exist, earrings exist, mobile apps exist, ML algorithms exist. But because the *combination* required seeing a connection that didn't exist in training data.

Why earrings specifically? Because women already wear them. Because they're positioned near major blood vessels in the ear. Because they're socially acceptable for continuous wear in a way that other wearables aren't. Because the form factor solves multiple problems simultaneously—sensing, power, aesthetics, social acceptability.

That insight required understanding:

- Women's health monitoring needs (domain knowledge)

- Wearable technology constraints (technical knowledge)

- Social acceptability patterns (cultural knowledge)

- Biosensor capabilities (scientific knowledge)

And then seeing how to combine them in a way that created value.

AI can optimize within existing patterns. It can't create new patterns by combining ideas from disparate domains in ways that don't exist in its training data.

6.5.2 A Conversational Commerce Agent

Recent work on conversational commerce agents illustrates another case where AI couldn't have designed the solution. Why?

Because it required:

Years of experience seeing what doesn't work. Building agent systems across multiple companies, using frameworks like LangChain, seeing their limitations in production, understanding why the imperative approach was fragile. That experience isn't in training data.

Purpose and intention. The drive to build something came from *wanting* to find a better way. From wanting to learn, to be challenged, to improve. AI optimizes for defined objectives. A gut feeling that something better was possible isn't an objective function you can train.

Willingness to break patterns. The standard approach was "write agent logic as code." Everyone was doing it. All the frameworks assumed it. Breaking from that pattern required believing that decades of programming wisdom—code is how you express logic—didn't apply here.

AI follows patterns in training data. Innovation requires breaking patterns.

6.5.3   When the Right Solution Isn't Rational

Here's something AI would never suggest because it's not rational: users don't want the fastest answer. They want to feel understood and in control.

I've seen this pattern play out in commerce agents: a system analyzes a user's query and returns optimal product recommendations in under a second. Technically impressive. Fast. Accurate.

Users hate it.

Why? Because it feels like the agent didn't even think about their question. They ask something like "I need a gift for my partner's birthday" and get instant results. It feels dismissive. Like the agent pre-decided without considering their specific situation.

The fix? Artificial delay. Progress indicators that signal the system is working through their request step by step.

Same results. A few seconds slower. Users love it.

An optimization algorithm would always prefer fewer interactions and faster responses. But humans don't experience AI as algorithms. They experience it as interaction. And interactions have social expectations.

You wouldn't trust a human consultant who answered complex questions instantly without appearing to think. You'd assume they weren't really considering your specific needs. Same with AI.

Being "right" isn't enough. Users need to feel understood and in control. That's a human insight about human psychology. Not something you can train an AI to discover by optimizing metrics.

6.6 The Care Factor: Why Machines Can't Be Accountable

I haven't had to take responsibility for a major AI system failure yet. But I know it will happen eventually.

When it does, here's what won't happen: the AI won't apologize. It won't feel bad. It won't learn from the emotional weight of having let people down. It won't work weekends to make things right because it cares about users.

Those are human responses. They matter.

When you build systems that serve millions of people, you carry responsibility for those people's experiences. Not as an abstract metric. As actual humans who trusted your system and got a bad outcome.

AI systems don't carry that weight. They can't. They're optimization engines. They adjust based on feedback loops, but they don't *care* about the outcomes.

That difference matters when things break. When users are frustrated. When the stakes are high.

Humans fix things at 3am not because we have to, but because we care. Because we feel responsible. Because these are our users, our product, our reputation.

You can't train that. It's not a capability gap that will be solved with better models. It's fundamental to what it means to be a tool versus what it means to be accountable.

6.7 Reading the Room: Context That Can't Be Documented

I've learned to adjust my approach in meetings based on signals that never make it into meeting notes.

Someone says "That's interesting" with a specific tone that means "I hate this but I'm being polite."

Someone asks a clarifying question that's actually a veiled objection: "How would this work with our existing architecture?" Translation:

"This breaks everything we've built."

Someone is unusually quiet. That either means they're thinking deeply or they're checked out. You can tell which by body language, by whether they're taking notes, by their history in previous meetings.

The VP leans forward. That means they're engaged. Leans back with arms crossed means you're losing them. Starts checking phone means you've already lost them.

These signals guide how I present ideas, when to slow down for explanation, when to skip details, when to pivot to address unspoken concerns.

None of this is in Slack transcripts or meeting recordings. It's read in real-time based on years of human interaction. It's applied with judgment about what matters in this specific moment with these specific people.

Could AI learn this? Maybe, with cameras analyzing body language, audio analyzing tone, training on thousands of meetings with labeled outcomes.

But even then: I adjust my approach not just based on what I observe, but based on what I care about. Do I want to win this argument or build consensus? Do I want to push my solution or find the best solution? Do I want credit or do I want the team to succeed?

Those are value judgments. They require caring about things beyond optimizing for a defined metric.

6.8   What This Actually Means

Let me be straight about what these limitations imply.

6.8.1   The Limitations Aren't Temporary

Some of AI's current limitations will be solved. Context windows will keep expanding. Models will get better at long-term planning. Error rates will decrease. Costs will fall.

But three fundamental limitations aren't going away:

AI can't care. It optimizes for whatever objective function you give it, but it doesn't have stake in outcomes beyond that function. It doesn't feel responsibility. It doesn't work harder because it cares about users.

AI can't innovate beyond its training. It can recombine existing patterns in sophisticated ways, but it can't create genuinely novel approaches that require breaking patterns or combining ideas from domains that aren't represented together in training data.

AI can't judge what matters. It can optimize defined metrics, but it can't determine which metrics are right, what trade-offs to make between competing values, when being technically correct is socially wrong.

These aren't bugs. They're inherent to how AI works. And they're exactly where human value remains.

6.8.2 The Gap Is Actually Good News

The gap between AI hype and AI reality frustrates me when it poisons markets and creates skepticism about real capabilities.

But the gap itself? The fact that AI can't do everything? That's good news for humans.

It means the work that matters—the judgment calls, the novel solutions, the caring about outcomes—remains human work. Not just for now, but fundamentally.

It means adapting to AI doesn't require becoming more like machines. It requires becoming more human—more creative, more caring, more strategic, more focused on problems machines can't solve.

The Humane AI Pin and Neo robot will fail not because AI isn't powerful, but because they tried to replace human capabilities with AI capabilities. They ignored the gap.

The products that will succeed are those that use AI to amplify human capabilities. That put AI's strengths (processing speed, pattern recognition, tireless execution) in service of human strengths (judgment, innovation, accountability, care).

That's not a consolation prize. That's the actual opportunity.

6.9 Why I'm Telling You This

I build these systems. I see what they can do. I also see what they can't do and never will be able to do.

When I tell you AI has fundamental limitations, I'm not diminishing AI's capabilities. I'm being precise about them. Understanding limitations is just as important as understanding capabilities.

When you know both, you can position yourself correctly. You stop worrying about AI doing everything and start focusing on the things only humans can do.

You stop competing with AI on AI's terms—speed, memory, breadth of knowledge—and start competing on human terms—judgment, creativity, accountability, care.

You stop seeing AI as a threat and start seeing it as a tool that makes the uniquely human work more valuable.

The next chapter explores exactly what those uniquely human skills are. Not in abstract terms, but in concrete, learnable capabilities.

Because understanding what AI can't do tells you where to focus. But you still need to know *how* to build those capabilities.

That's what comes next: the skills that remain irreplaceable, and how to develop them deliberately.

Chapter 7

Skill #1: Judgment Over Execution

7.1 The Obsessed Coder

Early in my career, I was obsessed with finding creative ways to solve problems. But I was only paying attention to immediate results—getting the task done, without understanding time complexity, memory usage, or even how maintainable my code was.

I worked alone for years. Like a mad scientist in a lab, writing code without version control. Even at companies with multiple employees, we'd pass projects between people sequentially—somebody starts with some code, someone else takes the project and continues, but never at the same time. No Git. No collaboration. Just individual execution.

My value was simple: I could write code that worked. That was enough.

7.2 The Fast Shipper

Mid-career, I became known for something specific: speed. I was very fast at producing good-quality results. Not the best quality—I made lots of mistakes. But I could get a working product quickly.

"If you want something done fast, give it to Ivan."

I carried this into my personal life too. I cook fast and well. I clean fast and well. Speed became my identity.

This was when I learned that maintainability matters. That sometimes you don't want to go so fast. That even very small mistakes can be very costly.

7.2.1 The Cassandra Migration: When Fast Was Wrong

At RetailNext, we needed to migrate Cassandra data. No staging environment. I didn't have proper training. The recovery plan had never been tested.

I approached it the way I approached everything: move fast, get it done.

I wrote the migration script. Reviewed it quickly. Ran it in production.

There was a tiny mistake. The keyspace name was wrong.

I caught it fast—stopped the process within seconds. But the damage was already severe. Large-scale downtime. Customer-facing services offline. Data corruption that took months to fully restore.

A single character error. Caught almost immediately. Still catastrophic.

This taught me something fundamental: **judgment about when to move fast matters more than the ability to move fast.**

Some situations reward speed. Get a prototype working, ship a feature quickly, iterate rapidly. Speed creates value.

Other situations punish speed. Data migrations. Security changes. Financial transactions. Anything where mistakes compound or can't be easily reversed.

The skill isn't being fast. It's knowing when fast is right and when careful is right.

AI can execute fast. It can't judge when fast is appropriate.

7.3 The Strategic Thinker

For the past few years, I've realized what actually drives me: I want to learn, research, and teach.

I spend time discussing high-level strategies. Giving architectural feedback in code reviews. If we need something done fast, I know I can do it—even faster now with AI tools.

But that's not where my value lies anymore.

My value is in deciding what to build and why. In seeing connections others miss. In preventing mistakes before they happen. In bringing judgment to problems where the technical solution is clear but the right choice isn't obvious.

7.3.1 When Code Became Magic

I realized this working at my own startups, where you do everything yourself: infrastructure, backend, frontend. You quickly figure out that code is totally irrelevant. Your only focus is the actual product you're trying to build.

Video streaming for local TV news stations. Content management systems for political groups. Interactive video guides for hotels.

In all these cases, what mattered was meeting with the designer and stakeholders to understand what to build. The code to make it possible? That was just magic. A means to an end.

The hard work wasn't typing code. It was understanding the problem well enough to know what solution would actually work. Not technically work—anyone can make technology work. But work for the users, for the business, for the constraints we operated under.

That's judgment.

7.4 New Framing: Questions Matter More Than Answers

Let me show you how this works in practice with a framework I built for agent orchestration.

7.4.1 The Initial Problem

Here's what I was initially trying to solve: I wanted ML engineers to focus on writing and testing prompts for a conversational commerce agent. I didn't want them writing Java.

Simple problem, right? Build an abstraction layer so ML people can work in their domain without touching application code.

7.4.2 How the Problem Evolved

As I started building, the problem definition evolved: we need a framework that allows us to deploy agents fast and do A/B testing.

Now it's not just about abstraction. It's about velocity and experimentation. The business needs to iterate quickly, test different approaches, measure what works.

7.4.3 The Question I Ultimately Answered

What I ultimately built wasn't just "let ML engineers write prompts without Java." It was a portable library that can create and support different types of agents—not only commerce agents, but a bunch of small specialized agents that solve different tasks and can run in different clouds and backends.

The question evolved from "how do we abstract Java?" to "how do we make agent development portable, testable, and composable?"

That's problem framing. Starting with a surface problem, digging into what you're actually trying to achieve, and discovering that the real question is different—and more important—than what you initially asked.

AI can answer questions. It can't reframe them.

If I'd asked AI "how do I let ML engineers work without writing Java?" it would have suggested solutions to that specific question. It wouldn't have realized that the real problem was about deployment velocity, A/B testing, and multi-cloud portability.

Those insights came from understanding the business context, the team's capabilities, the organizational constraints, and the longer-term strategic needs. Context that wasn't in any prompt or training data.

7.5 Strategic Thinking: Seeing What AI Misses

7.5.1 The Over-Engineering Problem

This happens constantly: AI gives you an over-engineered solution. You ask it to simplify. Now the solution is inefficient.

Why? Because AI optimizes locally. It sees the immediate problem and generates the technically optimal solution for that problem in isolation.

But real systems aren't isolated. They exist in organizational contexts with constraints AI doesn't see.

7.5.2 Rust vs Python: When "Better" Doesn't Win

Everyone knows Rust is more performant than Python. Better memory safety. Better concurrency. Technically superior for systems programming.

So why did the ML industry choose Python?

The practical answer: Python's library ecosystem for ML is outstanding. Most data scientists and ML engineers already know Python. The learning curve for Rust is steep. Large corporations need engineers who can be productive immediately, not engineers who spend months learning a new language.

The technically superior solution didn't get adopted. The "worse" technical solution ships and delivers value.

I understand this intellectually. Adoption matters more than technical perfection. A good solution people will use beats a perfect solution people won't learn.

But I'm still struggling with this one. It doesn't compute for me emotionally.

Part of me knows the organization is right—shipping something imperfect that works is better than not shipping something perfect. But another part of me sees the technical debt accumulating, the performance left on the table, the elegance sacrificed for expediency.

This tension—between what's technically right and what's organizationally pragmatic—is where judgment lives. And honestly? I'm still learning to navigate it.

Maybe that's the point. Judgment isn't about having perfect answers. It's about recognizing the tradeoffs, understanding the constraints, and making decisions even when they frustrate your engineering sensibilities.

That's harder than it sounds.

7.5.3 Cloud Provider Politics

Sometimes organizations prefer a specific cloud provider not because it's better, but because investors have interests in it—discounts, partnerships, strategic relationships.

You might architect a system that works beautifully on AWS. But if your investors want you on Google Cloud for strategic reasons, your perfect AWS architecture is worthless.

AI doesn't understand investor relationships. It doesn't know about board dynamics or strategic partnerships or political considerations that constrain technical decisions.

Humans bring that context. We make decisions that account for realities beyond the technical domain.

7.6 Experience-Based Judgment

7.6.1 The Lambda Memory Crisis

At Evolv AI, we had a complex system: messages came through Pub/Sub, each message type triggered a specific Lambda function, and some Lambdas would trigger other Lambdas if needed.

Then things started failing. Messages piling up. Errors cascading. A chain reaction of failures spreading through the system.

This would be very complex for an AI to analyze. Too many moving parts. Too many potential failure points. Error logs showing symptoms, not causes.

With my experience, I figured it out quickly: one particular message type required slightly more memory than the Lambda was allocated. That one message type was failing, backing up, triggering retries, creating cascading failures across the system.

How did I know? Pattern recognition from having seen similar issues before. Not at Evolv—at previous companies. The symptoms looked familiar. The architecture pattern was similar to something I'd debugged years earlier.

I'd built an intuition: when you see cascading failures in event-driven systems with memory-constrained workers, check if certain message types are hitting memory limits.

That's not something you can train. It's accumulated wisdom from having debugged similar systems, having made similar mistakes, having seen similar failures.

AI can analyze logs. It can pattern-match against known issues. But it can't say "I've seen this before" based on experiences across different companies, different systems, different contexts that aren't documented anywhere.

7.6.2 "I've Seen This Go Wrong Before"

This happens regularly. Someone suggests an approach. It looks reasonable. AI might even recommend it based on common patterns.

But I've seen it fail. Not in theory. In production. At a previous company. In a way that wouldn't be obvious from reading documentation or analyzing code.

"We tried something similar in 2019. It looked good on paper but caused cascading failures under load. Here's why..."

That institutional knowledge—that pattern recognition across companies and years—is irreplaceable. It's not in any database. It's not in any codebase. It's in human memory, transmitted through experience, accumulated through failures.

7.7 What Humans Bring That AI Cannot

Let me be direct about what's happening here.

AI processes patterns in data. Humans experience reality.

We don't just interact with this three-dimensional world. We create it. We constantly evaluate it, improve it, give it meaning.

7.7.1 The Meaning Gap

AI can optimize code for performance. It can't tell you whether performance matters in this context. It can suggest the fastest algorithm. It can't tell you whether speed is the right optimization target.

Humans decide based on context, experience, judgment, wisdom, perspective, intuition, feelings, emotions, love. Not just patterns and data.

Consider a simple decision: should this feature be fast or should it feel responsive?

Those sound similar. They're not. Fast means minimizing latency. Responsive means providing feedback that makes users feel the system is working. Sometimes making something feel responsive requires making it technically slower—adding progress indicators, showing intermediate results, giving users something to interact with while processing happens in the background.

AI optimizes for fast. Humans understand that users want responsive.

That difference—between optimizing metrics and understanding what actually matters—is where human judgment remains essential.

7.7.2 Balance and Perspective

A business can't be run entirely by men or entirely by women. It eventually fails. It lacks perspective.

Same with AI. You can't run a business entirely on AI optimization. It lacks the human perspective that brings meaning, values, and judgment about what's worth optimizing for.

Diversity of thought creates better outcomes. Not just demographic diversity—though that matters too—but diversity in how we process information.

AI brings speed and pattern recognition. Humans bring context and meaning. Together, they're more powerful than either alone.

But you need both. AI without human judgment optimizes for the wrong things. Humans without AI move too slowly to compete.

7.8   The Evolution of Intellectual Challenge

Here's what I think about the future.

In the 1930s, human computers inverted 10x10 matrices by hand. That was intellectually challenging work that required focus, skill, and expertise.

In the 1990s, writing a binary search algorithm in C++ was intellectually challenging work that required understanding data structures, algorithms, and implementation details.

In the 2010s, concurrency became the major intellectual and practical challenge. Understanding race conditions, deadlocks, thread safety. Building systems that could scale horizontally. This required new ways of thinking about program execution.

In the 2020s—right now—the primary intellectual and engineering challenge has rapidly become integrating, managing, and assuring the reliability and ethics of AI and machine learning systems within complex software ecosystems. It's not just using AI. It's making it reliable, safe, trustworthy at scale.

In the 2030s, reviewing AI-generated code and bringing judgment about whether it's correct, maintainable, and appropriate will be the intellectually challenging work.

The challenge evolves every decade. But humans need to be intellectually challenged to thrive.

7.8.1 Humans Are Readers and Reviewers Now

Even if we're "just" code reviewers, we learn by reading and reviewing. We're improving ourselves intellectually. As long as we're challenged every day, we're growing.

This isn't a downgrade. It's transcendence.

You don't need to know how to code to make an app anymore—AI can do that. But learning how to code puts you at an advantage. The same way learning to read put humans at an advantage even though you don't strictly need literacy to survive.

We're not becoming obsolete. We're moving up the abstraction stack. From executing calculations to programming computers. From programming computers to directing AI. From directing AI to... whatever comes next.

Each step is transcendence, not extinction.

7.8.2 The Irony of Advantage

Here's the irony: the people who learn to code will have an advantage over those who don't, even in a world where AI does the coding.

Why? Because understanding how code works lets you judge whether AI-generated code is good. Understanding algorithms lets you recognize when AI is suggesting something that will scale poorly. Understanding system design lets you architect solutions that AI can implement but couldn't conceive.

The advantage isn't in execution anymore. It's in judgment informed by deep understanding.

7.9 How to Build This Skill

So how do you develop judgment? How do you move from execution-focused to judgment-focused?

7.9.1 Do Hard Things Without AI First

This seems counterintuitive. If AI can do it, why would you do it manually?

Because understanding how things work at a deep level builds intuition that informs judgment.

I can judge AI-generated code quality because I've written thousands of lines of code manually. I know what good code looks like, what patterns cause problems, what decisions create technical debt.

If you've only ever used AI to generate code, you lack the foundation to judge whether the code is good. You're blind to patterns that cause problems because you've never experienced those problems.

Do the hard work without AI sometimes. Not because it's more efficient—it's not. But because it builds the understanding that makes you valuable.

7.9.2 Study Failures, Not Just Successes

Most people study successful architectures, successful companies, successful strategies. That's useful but incomplete.

Study failures. Read post-mortems. Understand what went wrong and why. Build a mental library of failure patterns.

When someone suggests an approach, you'll recognize "I've seen something similar fail because..." That pattern recognition is invaluable.

My Cassandra migration disaster taught me more about judgment than a hundred successful migrations would have. Because failures expose where judgment matters.

7.9.3 Work Across Multiple Companies

Judgment develops faster when you see problems in different contexts.

Throughout my career at various organizations, I've encountered different technical stacks, different organizational dynamics, different constraints.

That breadth gives me pattern recognition. When I see a problem,

I can recognize patterns from previous companies. "We tried something similar at RetailNext and it failed because of X." "Evolv solved this by doing Y, which might work here too."

You can develop this through job changes, or through consulting, or through contributing to open source projects in different domains. What matters is exposure to different contexts, different constraints, different failure modes.

7.9.4 Maintain a Decision Journal

This is simple but powerful: write down significant decisions you make, the reasoning behind them, and what you expect the outcome to be.

Then, six months later, review the decision. What actually happened? Was your judgment correct? If not, why not? What did you miss?

This builds self-awareness about your judgment patterns. You start noticing where your judgment is reliable and where it's consistently wrong. You develop calibration—knowing when to trust your intuition and when to seek more information.

7.9.5 Find Mentors Who Think Differently

You need people who will challenge your judgment. Not people who always agree with you—that just reinforces your existing patterns. People who see problems differently, who have different experiences, who will say "I think you're wrong about this and here's why."

I learned this during my first year studying mathematics at Universitat Autònoma de Barcelona. We'd all sit at the cafeteria. When somebody had a conjecture, another would immediately say "You're wrong. Prove it." Or "Did you try the opposite?"

This wasn't hostile. It was intellectual rigor. The assumption was that your first idea is probably wrong, or at least incomplete. The way to strengthen it is to have someone attack it, force you to defend it, make you consider alternatives.

I've carried this practice through my entire career. When I have an architectural decision to make, I deliberately seek out people who will disagree. Not to validate my choice—to stress-test it.

"Here's what I'm thinking. Tell me why it won't work."

Those conversations force you to examine your reasoning, consider alternative perspectives, and develop more nuanced judgment.

I've learned as much from people who disagreed with my decisions as from people who validated them. Maybe more.

7.10   The Practical Framework

Here's how I approach judgment calls now:

Step 1: Question the Question. Before answering, make sure you're solving the right problem. The stated problem is often a symptom. The real problem is usually deeper.

Step 2: Consider Context Beyond Code. What organizational constraints matter? What political dynamics are relevant? What strategic priorities should inform this decision? Code exists in a business context. Ignore that context and your judgment will be wrong.

Step 3: Pattern Match Against Experience. Have I seen something similar? How did it play out? What failure modes should I watch for? Experience is your database. Query it.

Step 4: Optimize for Adoption, Not Perfection. The best technical solution that won't get adopted is worthless. A good solution that people will actually use creates value.

Step 5: Decide When to Be Fast vs When to Be Careful. Some decisions are reversible. Move fast. Some decisions are costly to reverse. Move carefully. Knowing which is which is judgment.

Step 6: Review and Learn. Six months later, was this decision right? What worked? What didn't? What will I do differently next time?

7.11 Why This Skill Matters More Now

In a world where AI handles execution, judgment becomes the differentiator.

Two engineers using the same AI tools will produce vastly different results. Not because one's AI is better—they're using the same models. But because one has better judgment about what to build, how to frame problems, when to trust AI suggestions and when to override them.

That judgment can't be automated. It requires understanding context that isn't in training data. It requires experience with failure modes that aren't documented. It requires caring about outcomes beyond what metrics capture.

Judgment is the skill that makes you irreplaceable.

Not because AI will never have judgment. But because judgment requires experiencing reality, accumulating wisdom through failures, understanding meaning beyond patterns.

You're not competing with AI on execution speed. You're providing the judgment that makes AI execution valuable instead of just impressive.

That's the shift. From "how fast can I type code?" to "what's the right thing to build and why?"

Master that shift, and AI makes you more valuable, not less.

The next chapter explores the second irreplaceable skill: creativity that breaks patterns. Because judgment helps you choose among known options. Creativity generates options that didn't exist before.

Both matter. Both are uniquely human. Both become more valuable as AI handles execution.

And both can be developed deliberately, if you know how.

Chapter 8

Skill #2: Creativity That Breaks Patterns

8.1 Why AI Can't Innovate

Let me explain how AI actually works, because understanding this reveals why it fundamentally can't innovate.

Models like Claude and GPT go through multiple training stages. First, pretraining: the model learns language patterns from massive amounts of text, using self-supervised learning to predict the next token. Then supervised fine-tuning: training on high-quality human responses. Finally, RLHF—Reinforcement Learning from Human Feedback—where human evaluators compare pairs of model outputs and indicate which is better. The model is then fine-tuned to generate responses that score high according to this reward model.

This creates an illusion that what AI generates is correct. Then comes agentic AI that validates further, adding more layers of pattern-following on top of pattern-following.

But you see what's happening here? We've been teaching a system to follow rules that humans think are correct. First based on text patterns, then based on rewards. If the result is plausible, it's okay for an AI.

This works for algorithmic thinking. But human innovation?

8.1.1 Humanity's Next Evolutionary Step

We stand at a threshold as significant as the discovery of fire. AI isn't just another tool—it's automation on steroids that will completely redefine how we think, work, and create.

For generations, much of human labor has been algorithmic: repetitive tasks, pattern recognition, stimulus-response loops, optimization for defined metrics. This kind of work has value, but it doesn't require our highest capacities.

AI has now taken over this algorithmic work—the pattern-following, the reward-optimizing, the plausible-response-generating. This isn't a loss; it's an emancipation. It frees humanity to take our next evolutionary step: to fully embrace what we do best when we transcend mere pattern-following.

Pattern-following works to solve 90% of solvable problems. But the crucial 10%—the problems that actually move things forward—need a different perspective that no one has tried before. They need the audacity to break patterns, create new possibilities, pursue ideas that seem impossible but sometimes change everything.

That's where human creativity remains irreplaceable.

8.2 How Humans Actually Innovate

We humans sometimes break our own patterns to innovate. We create crazy theories. Some create theories because they just want to publish, or for ego. And we're so stubborn that we try to make our theories right.

After squaring the circle—pursuing something impossible, being told we're wrong, persisting anyway—somebody else comes in and sees a new idea that can be applied somewhere else. Bingo! Innovation.

This process can't be trained. It's not rational. It's driven by stubbornness, ego, curiosity, the refusal to accept that something can't be done.

Let me show you what this looks like in practice.

8.2.1   The C++ Content Management System Nobody Wanted

Early in my career, I built a web content management system in C++.

Everyone said this was stupid. Web CMSs were built in PHP, Python, Ruby. Scripting languages that were easy to modify, easy to hire for, easy to maintain. Building one in C++ was stubborn. Big ego on my part.

Why did I do it? Because I believed it could be more efficient. Because I wanted the performance. Because I didn't accept that "this is how it's done" was a good enough reason to not try something different.

Almost everyone thought I was wrong. Only a few people supported the idea. But I persisted. Big ego, yes. But also genuine conviction that there was value in the approach.

What happened? That CMS evolved. I turned it into a Golang backend framework—a language supported by Google App Engine. It became the foundation for many political organizations and apps, for multiple startups. Still powers systems to this day.

Why? Because it was the most economically efficient solution. Running costs were a fraction of equivalent systems built in Rails or Django. For startups watching every dollar, that mattered enormously.

Was I right from the start? No. The original C++ version was too hard to maintain, too difficult to find engineers for. But the core insight—that efficiency matters, that there's value in challenging how things are "supposed" to be done—that was right.

The stubbornness led somewhere unexpected. Not to proving I was right about C++, but to discovering that economic efficiency could be a strategic advantage, that Golang could capture the performance benefits without the maintenance costs.

That's how innovation actually works. You pursue something for reasons that might be partly ego, partly curiosity, partly conviction. You're probably wrong about the specifics. But the act of pursuing it leads somewhere valuable that you couldn't have predicted.

AI can't do this. It's trained to follow patterns, to generate plausible responses, to optimize reward functions. It can't be stubborn about crazy ideas. It can't pursue something everyone says is wrong because it has ego and conviction.

8.3 Case Study in Creative Insight

Let me walk you through how the declarative agent framework came to be, because it illustrates how creative breakthroughs actually happen.

8.3.1 The Initial Thought

I was thinking about a declarative language specification that could compile to some binary form. Traditional compiler approach: high-level language $\rightarrow$ optimized binary. Make it fast, make it efficient.

But then I got stuck on a practical question: how do I store this? Locally? Do I ship the agentic model in compiled form to every service?

8.3.2 The Sudden Realization

Suddenly, I realized: actually, it doesn't need to be compiled into a form that humans can't understand. It would be even more practical if it could be version controlled.

If it's human-readable configuration, engineers can review changes. They can diff versions. They can understand what changed between deployments. You lose some performance optimization, but you gain operational clarity.

8.3.3 The Trigger

What triggered this realization? I discovered that in our environment, configuration changes have a very different and simplified deployment process compared to code changes.

Code deployment: multiple review stages, security scanning, integration testing, staged rollouts. Takes days or weeks.

Configuration deployment: validate against schema, push to config service, services reload. Takes minutes.

And that clicked. Like, of course! Configurations can even be memory state. We could update agents in real-time if we want. No deployment pipeline. No service restarts. Just update the configuration and the agent behavior changes immediately.

That insight—that configuration deployment is fundamentally faster and safer than code deployment—transformed the entire design.

I wasn't trying to optimize for speed. I was trying to solve a storage problem. But the constraint revealed a much more important opportunity.

8.3.4   Why AI Couldn't Suggest This

Could AI have suggested this approach? No, for several reasons:

First, the insight came from understanding the organization's specific deployment constraints. That organizational knowledge isn't in training data. AI doesn't know that configuration changes are fast while code changes are slow.

Second, the creative leap was connecting two unrelated domains: language design (compilers, specifications) and operational processes (deployment pipelines, configuration management). AI doesn't naturally connect across domains this way.

Third, the insight required recognizing that a disadvantage (human-readable means less optimized) was actually an advantage (human-readable means more maintainable). That kind of value inversion requires judgment about what matters in context.

AI optimizes within patterns. This required breaking the pattern of "compiled is better than interpreted."

8.4   The Incora Earring: Inverting Technology

The Incora Earring project illustrates a different type of creativity: inverting existing technology to create something new.

8.4.1 The Core Problem

We wanted to measure core body temperature accurately. Wrist-based wearables measure peripheral temperature, which varies with blood flow and environment. Chest straps are accurate but uncomfortable for continuous wear, especially sleeping. Rings are popular but still measure peripheral temperature.

The ear canal provides access to core body temperature. The challenge: how do you create a wearable that people will actually wear continuously, including during sleep?

8.4.2 Why Earrings?

First, practical: we needed the thermistor inside the body, not on the surface. An earring post goes through the piercing, positioning the sensor in the ear canal. Perfect for accurate core temperature measurement.

But then the creative leap: an earring can be like a Bluetooth headset, but instead of a receiver, it's a transmitter.

Actually, wait. Does it even need to be constantly transmitting? That requires lots of power. What if we only transmit when needed?

The insight: the earring only wakes up to record temperature and store it in memory. It uses the Bluetooth transmitter only when it's in the charging case and has full power available. Sync data from the charging case, not from the earring itself.

This solved multiple problems simultaneously:

- Power efficiency: No constant transmission means smaller battery

- Safety perception: Not constantly radiating reduces health concerns

- Form factor: Smaller battery means more elegant design

- Comfort: Lighter earring is comfortable for 24/7 wear

8.4.3   The Inversion Pattern

Notice what happened: I started with "Bluetooth headset" as a mental model. But then inverted it. Not "receive audio," but "transmit data." Then inverted again. Not "transmit constantly," but "store and sync."

Each inversion challenged an assumption: that wearables should transmit continuously, that real-time data is necessary, that smaller batteries mean less capability.

AI can't do this kind of systematic assumption-challenging. It would suggest Bluetooth transmission because that's the pattern for wearable devices. It wouldn't naturally ask "what if we don't transmit at all?" because that breaks the pattern.

8.5   Three Types of Creativity That AI Can't Replicate

8.5.1   Type 1: Conceptual Innovation

Seeing problems differently. Reframing entirely.

The declarative agent framework I built wasn't just "better agent infrastructure." It was "what if agent behavior is data, not code?" That conceptual reframing changed everything about how I approach agent development.

AI can suggest improvements within a framework. It can't suggest reframing the framework itself.

8.5.2   Type 2: Cross-Domain Synthesis

This is where my career path becomes an advantage.

I learned product recommendation systems at Jetlore and Deloitte— how to optimize product detail pages (PDPs) and product listing pages (PLPs) for different verticals. I learned experimentation platforms and agent-based systems at Evolv AI.

When I needed to build a conversational commerce agent, I immediately understood what to build. Not because I'd built commerce agents before—I hadn't. But because I could synthesize knowledge from two different domains: e-commerce optimization from Deloitte plus agent frameworks from Evolv.

AI is siloed by its training data. It knows e-commerce patterns. It knows agent patterns. But connecting them to create something new? That requires seeing across domains in ways that training doesn't enable.

This is why breadth of experience matters. Specialists know one domain deeply. Generalists connect multiple domains to create innovations that specialists wouldn't see.

8.5.3   Type 3: Purposeful Disruption

Sometimes innovation requires deliberately doing something "wrong."

Building a CMS in C++ was wrong according to industry practice. Using configuration instead of code for agent behavior breaks software engineering conventions about compiled performance. Storing data locally instead of transmitting breaks IoT assumptions about connectivity.

Each of these "wrong" choices created value by challenging assumptions everyone accepted.

AI follows best practices. It generates solutions that conform to established patterns. It can't deliberately break conventions because it's trained on those conventions.

Humans can say "I know this is how it's supposed to be done, but what if we did the opposite?"

8.6   My Creative Process: How Ideas Actually Emerge

People ask me how I come up with ideas. Here's my actual process:

8.6.1   Phase 1: Deliberate Exploration

I brainstorm with stakeholders, designers, product owners. This helps me gather all the information I need. I propose plausible solutions—and sometimes crazy ones.

I never say "this is impossible" or "it can't be done." To me, everything is possible. Even zero point energy. We simply need to use a different physics paradigm.

This isn't naive optimism. It's deliberate suspension of constraints. When you assume nothing is impossible, you explore solution spaces that others dismiss immediately.

8.6.2   Phase 2: Consider the Opposite

I do this naturally, but it's also trained behavior from my first year studying mathematics at Universitat Autònoma de Barcelona.

We'd sit in the cafeteria. Someone would have a conjecture. Another would immediately say "You're wrong. Prove it." Or "Did you try the opposite?"

This wasn't hostile. It was intellectual rigor. The assumption was that your first idea is probably wrong, or at least incomplete. The way to strengthen it is to have someone attack it, force you to defend it, make you consider alternatives.

I've carried this practice through my entire career. When I'm stuck on a problem, I deliberately consider the inverse. If I'm thinking "we need to transmit data constantly," I ask "what if we never transmit?" If I'm thinking "this needs to be compiled," I ask "what if it's not?"

Often, the opposite doesn't work. But considering it reveals constraints you weren't aware of, or opportunities you hadn't seen.

8.6.3   Phase 3: Let It Rest

When I get stuck, I don't force it. I let the problem rest. I walk. I sleep. I work on something else.

Then, without consciously thinking about it, the intuition flourishes. The solution appears, often while doing something completely unrelated.

This isn't magic. It's how human cognition actually works. Conscious analysis is sequential, logical, constrained by what we're explicitly considering. Unconscious processing makes connections we're not deliberately seeking, sees patterns across experiences, combines ideas from different contexts.

AI doesn't have this. It processes when prompted. It doesn't have insights while "sleeping" because it doesn't have continuous background processing that synthesizes experiences over time.

8.6.4 Phase 4: Discuss Again

After intuition provides a direction, I discuss the idea again. Deliberately with people who have completely opposite perspectives from my original thinking.

This either strengthens the idea—if it survives opposing viewpoints, it's probably solid—or reveals flaws I need to address.

Then I let it rest again. The cycle repeats until the solution feels right.

8.6.5 Why AI Can't Replicate This

This process requires:

- Tolerance for ambiguity (exploring without knowing the answer)

- Unconscious processing (background synthesis over time)

- Ego and stubbornness (pursuing ideas despite opposition)

- Social intelligence (gauging reactions, reading subtext)

- Value judgments (deciding what "feels right")

AI can generate ideas on demand. It can't pursue them with conviction across weeks or months, letting intuition develop, adjusting based on social feedback, persisting despite criticism.

8.7 Cultivating Creativity: Practical Approaches

So how do you develop creative capacity? Based on my experience:

8.7.1 Diverse Experiences Matter More Than Deep Expertise

Throughout my career at various organizations—from startups to enterprise companies—I've encountered different industries, different technical stacks, different organizational cultures.

This breadth is my creative advantage. When facing a problem, I can draw on patterns from retail analytics, experimentation platforms, content management systems, and e-commerce optimization.

Specialists know one domain deeply. That's valuable for execution within that domain. But innovation often comes from applying patterns from one domain to problems in another.

Build breadth deliberately. Work at different types of companies. Contribute to projects outside your primary expertise. Learn adjacent fields.

8.7.2 Cross-Functional Knowledge Creates Connections

I've done coding, infrastructure, machine learning, AI, leadership. This isn't resume padding—each role taught me different ways of thinking about problems.

As a coder, I think about implementation details and edge cases. As an infrastructure engineer, I think about reliability and scale. As an ML practitioner, I think about data and optimization. As a leader, I think about people and organizations.

When facing a technical problem, I can consider it from all these angles. Often, the creative solution comes from applying a perspective from one role to a problem in another.

8.7.3 Learn Outside Your Domain

I don't watch cable TV. I choose what I learn from. I spend significant time reading.

I read tech and business news. I'm subscribed to AI newsletters, follow scholars and researchers. I read arXiv papers, check LinkedIn for industry trends, follow startup news. I visit tech and science museums.

I watch Gaia, documentaries about history, science, technology.

Why does this matter? Because creative insights often come from unexpected connections. A historical pattern might illuminate a technical problem. A biological system might suggest an architectural approach. A physics concept might reframe a software challenge.

Has non-tech knowledge informed tech solutions? Probably subconsciously. I can't point to specific instances, but I know that breadth of knowledge creates more connection points for creative synthesis.

8.7.4 Discuss Ideas With Others

This is where I get creative inspiration most consistently. Not from solitary thinking, but from discussing ideas with others.

Different people see different aspects of problems. They bring different constraints, different priorities, different experiences. Those differences spark connections I wouldn't make alone.

I use AI the same way I use a co-worker—as a thinking partner. AI is really great at coming up with ideas. I ask it questions, challenge its suggestions, use its responses to refine my thinking.

But the key is that I'm driving the conversation. I'm framing the problem, evaluating the suggestions, making the creative leaps. AI provides raw material. I provide direction and judgment.

8.7.5 Cultural Perspective Matters

I moved from Barcelona to Silicon Valley. This cultural shift changed how I think about problems.

What may seem like a problem in one culture isn't a problem in another. This helps you think more abstractly and be more critical.

Example: At Deloitte in Madrid, I pushed to hire remote engineers—common practice in US software development, opens up talent pools quickly. They wouldn't allow it because of policy. Insurance could only cover workers at a specific physical workplace, the designated office. Doing otherwise would be a liability.

Few months after I left Deloitte and returned to the Bay Area, COVID hit. Everyone was forced to work from home. What a nonsense, if you think about it.

The cultural difference taught me: policies that seem immutable aren't. Constraints that seem absolute are often just conventions.

Europeans have lots of policy. Change is slow. They're scared to make changes. Americans make changes only if it drives revenue. Both perspectives can be good and disappointing at times.

Being outside both cultures—European living in America, American working in Europe—gives perspective that pure insiders lack.

Seek exposure to different cultures, different work environments, different ways of thinking about problems. That perspective enables creativity.

8.8 The Human + AI Creative Partnership

Here's what AI changes about creativity: it doesn't replace creative thinking. It accelerates exploration of creative ideas.

8.8.1 How I Use AI in Creative Work

When I have an architectural idea, I use AI to rapidly prototype variations. I describe the concept, ask for implementation approaches, generate code to test feasibility.

This is dramatically faster than solo implementation. What used to take days—sketching out an idea, implementing a prototype, testing whether it works—now takes hours.

But notice what's happening: I'm generating the creative ideas. I'm framing the problems. I'm making the strategic choices. AI is accelerating the exploration phase, letting me test more variations more quickly.

8.8.2   AI as Thinking Partner

I also use AI as a thinking partner during the ideation phase. "Here's what I'm considering. What am I missing? What's the opposite approach? What could go wrong?"

AI generates perspectives I might not consider. Not because they're more creative than what I'd think of, but because they're faster to access than searching my memory or discussing with colleagues.

The key: I'm critically evaluating everything AI suggests. I'm looking for the useful insight buried in plausible-sounding but ultimately wrong suggestions. I'm using AI as raw material for creative synthesis, not as the source of creativity itself.

8.8.3   The Combination Is Powerful

Human creativity + AI execution is more powerful than either alone.

Humans alone can innovate but slowly. AI alone can execute but within existing patterns. Together: humans provide creative direction, AI accelerates implementation, humans evaluate results, cycle repeats rapidly.

This is the partnership that makes you more valuable, not less. You're not competing with AI on execution speed. You're using AI to multiply the impact of your creative ideas.

8.9   Why Creativity Can't Be Automated

Let me be direct about why creativity remains uniquely human:

Creativity requires caring about outcomes beyond defined metrics. I built the C++ CMS partly from ego, partly from conviction that efficiency mattered. AI doesn't have ego or conviction. It optimizes metrics you give it.

Creativity requires tolerating uncertainty. You pursue ideas without knowing if they'll work. You explore dead ends. You persist despite criticism. AI generates responses based on probability distributions. It doesn't "pursue" anything with uncertainty over time.

Creativity requires learning from failure across contexts.
My breadth across companies lets me recognize patterns others miss.
AI learns from training data. It doesn't accumulate experiences across
different organizational contexts and synthesize them later.

Creativity requires breaking your own rules. You have to
recognize when the patterns that usually work don't apply. When the
"right" way is wrong. When the opposite of best practice is what's
needed. AI follows patterns. It can't deliberately violate them.

Creativity requires unconscious processing. The best insights
come while walking, sleeping, doing something unrelated. Your brain
makes connections in the background. AI processes when prompted. It
doesn't have insights between sessions.

These aren't limitations that better training will solve. They're
fundamental to what makes human cognition different from pattern
recognition.

8.10   The 10% That Matters

Remember the 90/10 rule: pattern-following solves 90% of problems.
AI will get increasingly good at that 90%.

But the 10%—the problems that require new perspectives, that
need assumptions challenged, that demand stubborn pursuit of ideas
everyone says are wrong—that remains human work.

And that 10% is where value gets created. That's where innovations
emerge. That's where competitive advantages are built.

Don't compete with AI on the 90%. Learn to focus on the 10%
that requires creativity, judgment, and the uniquely human capacity to
break patterns and create something genuinely new.

The next chapter explores the third irreplaceable skill: connection
and context. Because creativity generates new ideas, judgment selects
among them, but relationships are what make ideas actually happen in
organizations.

All three skills matter. All three are uniquely human. All three become more valuable as AI handles execution.

And all three can be developed deliberately, if you commit to the practice.

Chapter 9

Skill #3: Connection and Context

9.1   Why Human Brains Need Other Human Brains

There's something remarkable that happens when humans work together that AI can't replicate, and neuroscience is beginning to understand why.

When people collaborate on tasks—solving problems, making music, teaching students—their brains begin to synchronize. Not metaphorically. Literally. Neural oscillations in one person's brain start to align with neural oscillations in another's brain. This phenomenon, called neural synchrony or brain-to-brain coupling, has been measured across multiple studies using EEG, fMRI, and other neuroimaging techniques.

Research shows that greater neural synchrony correlates with better performance on collaborative tasks[35], stronger interpersonal connection, and more effective communication. When couples work together on problems, their brains show gamma-wave synchronization that doesn't appear when strangers attempt the same tasks[36]. When teachers and students are engaged in learning, their brain activity synchronizes—and the degree of synchrony predicts how well students retain the material.

This isn't just correlation. The synchrony appears to be functional. People whose brains synchronize better perform collaborative tasks more effectively. Teams with higher inter-brain synchrony solve problems

---

[35] Kinreich et al., "Brain-to-Brain Synchrony during Naturalistic Social Interactions", 2017.

[36] Reinero, Dikker, and Van Bavel, "Inter-brain Synchrony in Teams Predicts Collective Performance", 2021.

faster and more accurately than teams with lower synchrony.

Here's what matters for our discussion: this neural coordination emerges from face-to-face human interaction. It develops through shared attention, joint action, mutual gaze, and the subtle coordination of verbal and nonverbal signals. It strengthens with familiarity, trust, and collaborative history.

AI can't participate in this. It doesn't have neural oscillations to synchronize. It can't engage in the continuous, dynamic coordination that human brains perform automatically during interaction.

9.1.1 What This Means for Work

Stanford researchers studying human-centered AI emphasize that as AI takes over transactional tasks, the value of work increasingly shifts to what Jennifer Aaker calls "authentically human" capacities: genuine connection, empathetic communication, and the kind of collaboration where human brains coordinate in ways that create emergence—where the whole becomes greater than the sum of its parts[37].

AI optimizes. It makes us faster and more efficient. But it doesn't make us better in the ways that matter for complex human endeavors. Better, Aaker explains, means a doctor using AI insights to have more empathetic conversations with patients—rather than reducing interactions to mechanical transactions. Better is when AI frees us to spend more time on the human connections that create trust, facilitate learning, and enable the kind of collaboration that generates genuinely novel solutions.

As AI handles more tasks, human work becomes primarily about connection: building relationships that enable collaboration, establishing trust that allows for risk-taking, creating the social fabric that makes organizations function.

This isn't soft skill versus hard skill. This is the skill that determines whether anything actually gets done.

---

[37] Aaker, "Human First: Designing Artificial Intelligence That Elevates Us", 2024.

9.2 How I Built Trust at a New Role

When I joined a new organization in 2025, I faced a challenge common to all engineers entering large organizations: establishing credibility and trust quickly.

Let me show you what this looks like in practice.

9.2.1 The First Win: Three Weeks to Credibility

Within a few weeks of starting in January 2025, I delivered an admin console—an internal tool that had been a recognized need but never prioritized.

I built it in three weeks. During onboarding. While learning the systems, meeting people, understanding the organization.

I demoed it to the larger team in my second or third week.

That demo established credibility faster than months of meetings could have. Not because the tool was technically complex—it wasn't. But because it solved a real problem that everyone recognized, and I delivered it when nobody expected delivery.

Trust doesn't come from credentials or titles. It comes from proven capability. From showing that when you say you'll build something, you build it. When you identify a problem, you solve it.

That first win opened doors. When I later proposed the declarative agent framework, people listened. Not because the idea was obviously good—it was unconventional, unproven, risky. But because I'd demonstrated that I could deliver.

9.2.2 The "No Bullshit" Approach

Here's what else built trust: I don't talk about small things or personal issues with coworkers. I talk tech with vision.

This isn't because I'm antisocial or because personal relationships don't matter. It's because at this scale, executives and directors are overwhelmed with noise. Small talk. Politics. Personal grievances. Complaints about processes.

129

When I get time with decision-makers, I use it to discuss ideas that matter. Technical approaches that could transform how we build systems. Strategic directions that align with business priorities. Problems worth solving and solutions worth pursuing.

They trust me because I don't waste their time. Because when I bring something to them, it's substantial. Because I've thought through the implications, understood the constraints, and have concrete proposals rather than vague suggestions.

This is relationship-building through respect for their time and attention. Through demonstrating that conversations with me are valuable, not just pleasant.

9.2.3   Paving the Way: Building Coalitions

When I wanted to build the declarative agent framework, I didn't go straight to executives for approval. I paved the way.

First, I presented the idea to a few team members. Got their input. Refined the concept. Built initial support.

Then I worked my way up through levels of leadership, building alignment at each stage.

At each level, the presentation was casual but substantive. I wasn't asking for permission—I was building shared understanding. Letting them see the vision, ask questions, raise concerns. Incorporating their feedback into the approach.

By the time we needed formal approval, it wasn't a decision. It was a confirmation of something that already had organizational momentum.

This is how things actually get done in large companies. Not through formal processes and approval chains, but through building coalitions, establishing shared vision, and creating alignment before you need it.

9.2.4   The "Next Rodeo" Philosophy

One of my former colleagues, Cihan Ucar who was my CTO at Clovers, taught me something important about relationships in tech: "Today

I'm your CTO, but who knows—in our next rodeo you'll be my CTO."

This captures a fundamental truth about Silicon Valley relationships: roles are temporary, but relationships persist. The engineer you mentor today might be the VP who hires you tomorrow. The peer you collaborate with at one company becomes your director at another. The person reporting to you now might be your boss in five years.

This isn't about manipulation or networking for advantage. It's about recognizing that we're all very experienced professionals who play different roles in different contexts. Mutual respect and genuine collaboration matter more than hierarchy.

When I work with people, I work with them. I'm there for them 200%. Not because I expect reciprocity, but because that's how you build relationships that last beyond any single role or company.

People trust me because they know that when I commit to something, I follow through. When they need help, I help. When we're on the same boat, I'm rowing.

That trust compounds. It becomes reputation. It opens opportunities. Not through calculated networking, but through genuine collaboration that creates mutual value.

9.3 Reading the Room: What AI Can't See

Here's a skill that matters more than people realize: reading unspoken signals in meetings.

9.3.1 What I Actually Look For

When I'm in a meeting—especially a meeting where I'm proposing something or need buy-in—I'm watching several things simultaneously.

First: attention. Who's giving full attention? Who's on their laptop with the screen angled away? Who's checking their phone under the table?

This tells me immediately who's engaged and who's not. If key decision-makers aren't paying attention, it's the wrong meeting. I need to stop, reschedule, or pivot to something that will capture their attention.

Second: body posture. Are they leaning forward or back? Arms crossed or open? Hands visible or hidden?

Leaning forward signals engagement. Leaning back with arms crossed signals skepticism or resistance. Hands on the table signals openness. Hands hidden signals discomfort or defensiveness.

Third: eye contact and blink rate. How often are they blinking? Where are they looking?

Rapid blinking can signal stress or cognitive overload—you're going too fast or the concept is too complex. Slow, steady blinking signals comfort and processing. Eyes darting around signal distraction or disengagement.

Fourth: verbal cues that contradict content. Someone says "That's interesting" but their tone is flat. Someone asks a "clarifying question" that's actually a veiled objection.

These signals tell you what people really think versus what they're willing to say directly.

9.3.2   How I Adjust

If I notice key people aren't engaged, I adjust immediately. Sometimes that means speeding up—get to the punch line faster. Sometimes it means slowing down—they're not ready for where I'm going, need more context.

If I see skepticism building, I address it directly. "I'm seeing some concerns. What questions do you have?" Better to surface objections now than discover them after the meeting when they block your proposal.

If I realize it's the wrong time—people are distracted, preoccupied, not ready to engage—I schedule another meeting. No point pushing forward when the conditions aren't right for the conversation you need.

This is why Zoom meetings are harder than in-person. You lose most of these signals. You can see faces but not body language. You can't tell if someone's checking email or taking notes. The subtle coordination that happens naturally in physical space gets disrupted.

AI can't do this. Not because the technology can't recognize facial expressions or measure engagement—those capabilities exist. But because the skill isn't pattern recognition. It's contextual interpretation.

The same body language means different things in different contexts with different people. Someone leaning back with arms crossed might be skeptical. Or they might be comfortable and thinking deeply. Or they might be cold because the conference room AC is too high.

You know which by reading the totality of signals, by understanding this person's baseline behavior, by sensing the room's energy, by having built relationships that let you interpret ambiguous signals correctly.

That's human intelligence operating in social contexts. AI has pattern recognition. Humans have contextual understanding.

9.4 Navigating Politics: The Unwritten Rules

Every organization has unwritten rules. Politics, if you want to call it that. But I prefer to think of it as understanding how decisions actually get made versus how the org chart says they should get made.

9.4.1 Getting Engineer Buy-In First

When I wanted to build the declarative agent framework, managers and directors were initially skeptical. Not because the idea was bad, but because there were other priorities. Always more urgent things than foundational infrastructure.

So I went to the engineers actually doing the work. Showed them the prototype. Explained how it would make their lives easier. Got them excited about the possibilities.

Once engineers wanted it, managers couldn't ignore it. When your team is asking for a tool, you find a way to prioritize it.

This is politics, but not the negative kind. It's understanding that adoption happens bottom-up as much as top-down. That engineers who will use the tool daily have more influence than executives who will never touch it.

9.4.2 Anticipating Needs

Something else I did: I anticipated the need before it was urgent.

I planted the idea early. "Here's something we might need in six months." Let it sit in the back of people's minds. Mentioned it occasionally. Showed incremental progress.

By the time we actually needed it, it wasn't a new idea requiring explanation and buy-in. It was an obvious solution to a problem everyone recognized.

This is organizational intelligence. Understanding that humans resist new ideas but embrace ideas they've been thinking about for a while. That you can't force adoption, but you can create conditions where adoption feels natural.

9.4.3 What's Not Written Anywhere

Here's knowledge that exists nowhere in documentation but matters enormously:

Which teams have political conflicts from past reorganizations. Which executives care deeply about specific issues that aren't in their formal responsibilities. Which partnerships have contractual constraints that limit technical options. Which decisions from 2019 still affect architecture choices today.

This institutional memory lives in people's heads. It gets transmitted through conversations, through mentorship, through stories people tell about what happened last time someone tried X.

AI doesn't have access to this. Even if you fed it every Slack message and design doc, it wouldn't understand what matters and what's historical artifact.

Humans who've been through the organization's history carry context that makes them invaluable navigators. They can tell you "we tried that in 2021 and here's why it failed" or "that team seems like the right partner but actually there's tension from a previous project" or "this executive will support this if you frame it as customer experience, but not if you frame it as technical efficiency."

That organizational intelligence can't be learned from documents. It's learned through relationships, through being part of the organization's story, through accumulated experience watching how decisions play out.

9.5 Teaching and Mentorship: What AI Can't Provide

At Clovers, two engineers from different teams specifically asked to have regular meetings with me. They wanted mentorship beyond technical skills.

9.5.1 What They Actually Wanted to Know

Their questions weren't about code. They were about navigating careers:

Is the corporate world better than startups? What should I learn next? How can I improve my communication? How do I know when to change jobs? How do I negotiate compensation? How do I know if I'm on the right path?

These are questions AI can answer with information. But information isn't what they needed.

9.5.2 What I Provided

I provided real experience. The feelings. How to actually deal with situations firsthand.

It's easy to say "just communicate clearly" or "know your worth when negotiating." It's different to live it. To feel the anxiety of asking for more money. To experience the awkwardness of giving negative feedback to a peer. To navigate the uncertainty of choosing between a stable corporate job and an exciting but risky startup.

I shared stories. Not just "here's what to do" but "here's what happened to me when I did X, and here's what I wish I'd known."

I provided judgment based on understanding them as individuals. The advice that works for one person doesn't work for another. Some people thrive in structured corporate environments. Others wither there and need startup chaos to be energized.

AI can provide general advice. Humans provide contextualized wisdom that accounts for who you are, what drives you, what your constraints are.

9.5.3   The Learning That Happens

Most importantly: they learned by watching me work. Not from explicit instruction, but from observation.

How I approach technical problems. How I navigate disagreements with stakeholders. How I prioritize when everything feels urgent. How I decide when to push hard and when to let something go.

This is how humans actually learn complex skills. Not from instruction manuals, but from apprenticeship. From working alongside someone more experienced and absorbing not just what they do but how they think.

AI can provide information. It can't model the messy reality of professional judgment in context. It can't show you how decisions feel, how uncertainty gets managed, how experience shapes intuition.

As a result of our mentorship relationship, I saw their careers improve. They walked their own paths. They thrived.

That's what human mentorship provides: not just information, but the confidence and context to act on it effectively.

9.6   My Evolution: From Solo Coder to Collaborative Leader

Let me tell you about my own journey with relationships and leadership, because it wasn't natural or easy.

9.6.1 The Demoscene: First Leadership Experience

In my twenties, I taught programming and computer graphics at an academy in Barcelona. Small classes—five or six students each time. Different groups, different ages.

For the end-of-course project, I tried something unusual: I got them to work together as a team. We'd create a demo—a real-time audiovisual presentation—and present it at the Euskal Party demoscene contest.

This was 1996. I was young, barely older than some of my students. The demoscene was this underground computer art movement where programmers, musicians, and artists competed to create impressive real-time graphics and sound within strict technical constraints.

That was my first experience leading a team. Not managing engineers at a company, but coordinating creative people with different skills toward a shared goal. Learning to balance individual contributions with collective vision. Understanding that the leader's job is to enable others' work, not to do everything yourself.

We competed at Euskal Party from 1994 to 1996. Some projects succeeded. Some failed. But I learned something fundamental: creating things collaboratively is different from creating things alone. More complex. More frustrating. But capable of results no individual could achieve.

9.6.2 The Long Gap

It wasn't until many years later, after I'd moved to Silicon Valley, that I led a team that large again. At Jetlore, I managed five people—QA engineers, designers, software engineers—building recommendation systems.

This was harder than the demoscene experience in some ways. Corporate context, not creative freedom. Deadlines and business priorities, not artistic vision. Multiple stakeholders with conflicting requirements.

9.6.3 What Leadership Actually Requires

The hardest part has always been communication. Not just language barriers—though those exist—but culture, different personal priorities, different work styles.

Remote employees in different timezones are particularly challenging. You have to be mindful of their lives. As a leader, you want to be the one adapting to their schedule, not forcing them to adapt to yours.

If teams are split across large timezone gaps, you ideally want them working on completely different problems or services. Otherwise, the coordination overhead becomes prohibitive.

For large organizations, you want a manager in each major timezone. Not because remote management can't work, but because daily synchronous collaboration matters for team cohesion.

9.6.4 The Surprise: They'll Produce Something

Here's what surprised me about leadership: whether you do it well or poorly, the team is going to produce something.

Sometimes it solves the problem. Sometimes it creates more problems.

The leader's job isn't to do the work. It's to create conditions where the team can do their best work. To remove obstacles. To provide context. To make decisions when needed. To stay out of the way when not needed.

9.6.5 Ownership Over Micromanagement

The most important lesson: you want to give people ownership. Micromanagement is the worst thing you can do.

Everyone wants to feel empowered. Even if they're naive. Especially if they're naive.

New engineers often have more creative ideas than experienced ones because they haven't learned all the reasons something "can't" be done. Your job as a leader is to protect that creativity while adding the judgment that comes from experience.

You don't tell them "that won't work." You say "here are the constraints" and let them figure out solutions. Sometimes they surprise you. Sometimes you were wrong about what's possible.

The relationship works when people feel ownership over their work. When they can point to something and say "I built that, I made those decisions, I'm responsible for this."

That's when people thrive. That's when they produce their best work. That's when they grow.

9.7 The Translator Role: Bridging Technical and Business

One of the most valuable relationship skills I've developed is translation—moving between technical and business contexts, helping each side understand the other.

9.7.1 The Business-to-Engineers Direction

This one is easier. Engineers want to work for their customers. They want to see the impact of their efforts. They want to solve real problems.

When you translate business needs to engineers, you're giving them purpose. "Here's why this matters. Here's who it helps. Here's the problem we're solving."

Engineers respond to that. Even if their immediate customer is another group of engineers, they want to know the chain: we build this so that team can do that so that users get this benefit.

The challenge is being transparent about priorities and tradeoffs. Engineers can handle complexity. What they can't handle is ambiguity about what matters and why.

9.7.2 The Engineers-to-Business Direction

This is harder. Much harder.

Business stakeholders often don't understand technology. And right now, with all the hype around Cursor and AI tools, they think everything can be done quickly and cheaply.

You can't fight the hype directly. If you say "no, AI can't do that," they think you're being resistant or you don't understand the technology.

Instead, you find common ground. You focus on the larger picture. You listen to what they actually need—which is often different from what they're asking for.

And you're transparent about what you've seen succeed and what you've seen fail. Not theoretical arguments, but concrete examples: "We tried this approach at my previous company and here's what happened."

Experience trumps theory. When you can say "I've built this before and here's what worked," people listen.

9.7.3 The Value of Translation

Why does this matter so much? Because organizations fail when engineering and business can't communicate effectively.

Engineers build the wrong things because they don't understand business priorities. Business makes commitments that engineering can't fulfill because they don't understand technical constraints.

The people who can bridge that gap—who can translate business needs into technical requirements and technical capabilities into business opportunities—become invaluable.

It's not about being the smartest technical person or the best business strategist. It's about being the person both sides trust to represent their interests accurately.

That's a relationship skill, not a technical one.

9.8 Building Relationship Capital Deliberately

Let me be practical about how to develop this skill.

9.8.1   Be There 200%

When you commit to working with someone, be all in. Not half-engaged while thinking about your next project. Fully present, fully committed.

This means:

- Responding to messages promptly (not instantly, but reliably)

- Following through on commitments without reminders

- Helping when asked, even when it's not your responsibility

- Showing up prepared for meetings, having done the work

People remember who shows up. They remember who they can count on. That memory becomes trust, and trust becomes relationship capital.

9.8.2   Bring People With You

I try to bring people I trust wherever I go. Not because I need familiar faces, but because I know what they're capable of and they know how I work.

When you build strong collaborative relationships, you want to preserve them. The people you work well with become more valuable over time as you develop shared context and understanding.

This isn't nepotism. It's recognizing that great working relationships are rare and worth maintaining.

9.8.3   Build Relationships Before You Need Them

Don't wait until you need someone's help to start building the relationship.

I presented the declarative agent framework idea to parallel teams before I needed their buy-in. Not because I was asking for anything, but because I wanted them to understand the direction.

When I later needed their support, the relationship already existed. The conversation was continuation, not cold start.

This applies to mentorship too. I mentor people not because I need something from them, but because helping others is valuable in itself. Years later, some of them end up in positions where they can help me. Not because I calculated that outcome, but because relationships compound over time.

9.8.4 Invest in Cross-Functional Relationships

Don't just build relationships within your function. Build them with product managers, designers, business stakeholders.

I've been very lucky to work with great product managers, designers, and stakeholders who are passionate about what they do and willing to learn about technology.

How do you build those relationships? Time and shared work. Being on the same boat. Building trust through collaboration.

The collaboration might start small. Helping them understand a technical constraint. Them helping you understand a user need. Those small collaborations create foundation for larger ones.

9.8.5 Always Be Willing to Help

This is simple but powerful: be willing to help opens many doors to future collaboration.

Someone asks a question in Slack. You could ignore it—not your problem. Or you could take five minutes to help.

Someone needs a code review. You could do the bare minimum. Or you could provide thoughtful feedback that helps them grow.

Someone is stuck on a problem. You could send them to documentation. Or you could spend thirty minutes helping them understand the underlying issue.

These small acts of help accumulate. They create a reputation. "Ivan is someone who helps." That reputation becomes relationship capital that compounds over time.

9.9 Why AI Can't Replace This

Let me be direct about why relationships remain irreplaceable as AI handles more tasks.

9.9.1 Trust Requires Accountability

When executives trusted my recommendation to build the declarative agent framework, they weren't just trusting the idea. They were trusting me.

If it failed, I would be responsible. Not abstractly responsible—personally responsible. They knew I would work nights and weekends to make it succeed. They knew I cared about the outcome beyond metrics.

AI can generate recommendations. It can't be accountable for them. When AI suggests something and it fails, who's responsible? The person who implemented it? The team that deployed it? The company that trained the model?

Human relationships are built on mutual accountability. We trust people because we know they'll own outcomes, fix problems, learn from failures.

9.9.2 Collaboration Requires Synchrony

Remember the neural synchrony research? Human brains coordinate during collaboration in ways that create emergence—collective intelligence that exceeds individual capacity.

That coordination happens through subtle social signals, shared attention, mutual adaptation. Through working together repeatedly until you develop intuition about how your collaborator thinks, what they'll suggest, where they'll struggle.

AI can participate in task completion. It can't participate in the neural synchrony that makes human collaboration genuinely creative and adaptive.

9.9.3 Growth Requires Human Modeling

The engineers I mentored at Clovers learned more from watching me work than from anything I explicitly taught.

That's how humans learn complex judgment: through observation and apprenticeship. Through seeing how someone more experienced handles ambiguity, makes tradeoffs, navigates politics.

AI can provide information. It can't model the lived experience of professional judgment. It can't show you what decisions feel like when you're uncertain. It can't demonstrate how experience shapes intuition over years.

9.9.4 Organizations Run on Relationships

Org charts show reporting structures. They don't show how work actually gets done.

Work happens through relationships. Through knowing who to ask for help. Through understanding whose buy-in you need. Through building coalitions that can move ideas forward.

AI can optimize processes. It can't build the relationships that make organizations function.

As AI handles more transactional work, the value of human work shifts entirely to relationships. Not despite AI, but because of it.

The work that remains is the work that requires trust, collaboration, context, and the uniquely human capacity to coordinate with other humans in ways that create collective intelligence.

9.10 The Path Forward

If you're worried about your value in an AI world, invest in relationships deliberately.

Build trust through delivery and accountability. Learn to read rooms and navigate politics. Develop the ability to translate between technical and business contexts. Mentor others and be mentored. Create relationship capital that compounds over time.

These aren't "soft skills." They're the skills that determine whether anything actually gets done.

Judgment tells you what to build. Creativity generates new possibilities. But relationships make it happen.

All three skills matter. All three are uniquely human. All three become more valuable as AI handles execution.

The next chapter explores the fourth skill—the meta-skill that makes all others possible: learning to learn. Because in a world where specific knowledge becomes obsolete rapidly, the ability to adapt is the only permanent advantage.

And that's what we explore next.

Chapter 10

Skill #4: Learning to Learn (Meta-Skill)

10.1 The Only Permanent Advantage

I'm writing this book at 48 years old. I finished my Master's degree in Computer Science with AI/ML specialization a few months ago. I got my Bachelor's degree in Computer Science just two years before that, at 46.

While working full-time. Building production systems, leading projects, filing patents.

Why am I telling you this? Not to brag. But to establish something fundamental: **it's never too late to learn what you need to learn.**

More importantly: in a world where specific knowledge becomes obsolete rapidly, the ability to learn is the only advantage that never depreciates.

Programming languages come and go. Frameworks rise and fall. AI models that are state-of-the-art today will be outdated next year. Every specific skill you have right now has a half-life.

But your ability to learn new skills? That's permanent. That's what makes you valuable regardless of which wave of technology arrives next.

Let me show you how this works in practice.

10.2 Why I Got Degrees at 46

People ask why I went back to school in my mid-forties. The surface answer: I needed credentials to work in ML research in industry.

But the deeper answer: I wanted to work in academic research and teaching. I realized you can't just write papers without credentials. During my career, I'd worked with many PhDs and ABD candidates. I always admired the clarity and communication skills of the ones who actually finished their dissertations.

I knew that if I wanted to get there eventually, it wouldn't be only through writing books and mentorship. It required rigorous work in explaining complex topics in papers and being able to defend them.

Also, I wasn't an engineer anymore. I was becoming a computer scientist specializing in AI and machine learning. That identity shift required formal foundation, not just practical experience.

10.2.1 How I Actually Did It

The mechanics matter because people think it's impossible to get degrees while working full-time. It's not impossible. It's structured.

I had a schedule and followed it strictly. At least 10 hours during weekdays—one hour in the morning, one hour in the afternoon. On weekends, depending on family responsibilities, I'd go all day if possible. But at minimum, I maintained the two hours daily even on weekends.

This wasn't negotiable. Not "I'll study when I have time." Scheduled time, protected time, consistent time.

Here's what made it work: I had purpose. I knew where I wanted to get, even though it was far away. Everything made sense because I understood why I was doing it.

10.2.2 What Was Actually Hard

The beginning was the hardest part. Staring at a two-year Bachelor's program and a subsequent Master's program while working full-time felt impossible. "How can I manage my personal life too?"

Those doubts came during planning, before I'd even started. Once I began, momentum carried me forward.

What surprised me: learning at 46 was actually easier than I thought. Specifically, things like Calculus II and Multivariable Calculus that had been intimidating in my twenties. I realized we create our own blockages growing up. That I'd lacked mentorship at a time when I needed it most.

Age gave me advantages: I knew why I was learning each concept. I could connect new knowledge to decades of practical experience. I had developed learning techniques that my 20-year-old self didn't have.

10.2.3 The Crisis Moment

One specific example: I took a Machine Learning course at UT Austin during my Master's program. The theoretical and practical test required lots of practice and preparation time.

The test could only be done during a particular week. The curriculum was very extensive—too extensive, honestly. And I got sick. The test couldn't be postponed.

I studied every day like crazy while sick. I grouped the types of questions and problems, broke the curriculum into more manageable blocks. Developed frameworks for understanding related concepts together rather than trying to memorize everything individually.

It didn't turn out as well as I would have wished. But it was good enough. And the process of studying under pressure taught me more about my learning capacity than easier courses did.

That's when I knew I could do this. Not perfectly, but adequately. And adequate while working full-time beats perfect while being a full-time student.

10.3 My Learning System: The Practical Details

People want to know: how do you actually stay current with technology that's changing exponentially?

10.3.1 Information Sources That Matter

I subscribe to several AI newsletters:

- Deeplearning.AI—Andrew Ng's newsletter on AI developments

- TLDR AI—daily summary of AI news

- AI Breakfast—morning briefing on latest developments

- ACM Learning—academic perspective on computing advances

- Bruce Schneier's monthly newsletter—security and broader tech implications

I follow people working in the industry on LinkedIn, trying to avoid marketing as much as possible. Real practitioners sharing real work, not consultants selling hype.

I read papers every week. Specifically, I read abstracts and use AI to help me skim for relevance. Then I deep-dive on papers that matter to what I'm building or learning.

This isn't passive consumption. I'm actively looking for:

- What problems are people solving that I might face?

- What approaches are working in production?

- What's hype versus what has evidence?

- What's emerging that I should learn before I need it?

10.3.2 Learning While Building

Here's something crucial: you can learn while you build. You can learn a new skill, a new library, a new programming language. You can always find an excuse to directly apply something you want to learn while you're working or building something.

Example: I learned TypeScript in my free time while working at Evolv AI. It wasn't immediately necessary for my job. But I knew it would be useful eventually.

In my next role, I knew I could build the admin console quickly because I already knew TypeScript. That knowledge let me kick-start the project in just a few weeks instead of months.

Another example: At Clovers, we deliberately chose a Postgres client that wasn't fully supporting all our use cases but had the right implementation architecture. We chose it specifically to contribute to the open source project—to learn and get exposure to collaborating with other teams and companies with different needs but common technical ground.

And a failure that taught lessons: I built a Golang package to support the Metal Framework. This was novel at the time but was deliberately a way to force myself to learn the Metal API. The project didn't succeed commercially, but I learned Metal deeply. That knowledge informed other work later.

10.3.3   Building Feedback Loops

How do I know if I'm learning effectively? Three mechanisms:

First: Build projects to test understanding. You don't know if you've learned something until you've used it to create something. Reading about a concept isn't learning. Building with it is learning.

Second: Teach others to solidify learning. I try to teach colleagues as much as I can. Teaching forces you to understand concepts deeply enough to explain them clearly. When someone asks "why does this work this way?" and you can't answer, you've found a gap in your understanding.

Third: Discuss with colleagues constantly. I engage with people who know more than I do about specific topics. They correct my misconceptions. They show me better approaches. They challenge my understanding.

And I measure progress by comparing my work and understanding with where I want to get, constantly evaluating.

10.4 The Learning Mistake That Blocked Me

Let me tell you about a significant mistake I made for years that hindered my learning.

I used to create preconceptions about how something should work before I learned it. This created a barrier that didn't let me learn the concept because I was always thinking the professor was wrong, that there should be a better way.

I was always trying to go a few steps ahead of the teacher. And this actually blocked my learning process.

Once I realized this big mistake, I was able to pay full attention to what I was learning. I'd learn the concept as presented, test my knowledge to make sure I understood it correctly, and *then* think about my original hypothesis. Where was I right? Maybe that's an opportunity for research. Where was I completely wrong? What did I miss?

This shift—from "I know better" to "let me understand first"—dramatically accelerated my learning.

The irony: my younger self, who thought he knew everything, learned slower than my older self who admits he doesn't know and needs to learn properly.

10.5 What Multiple Waves Reveal

Looking back at the four waves of supposed obsolescence I've lived through, a meta-pattern emerges.

10.5.1 Cycles, Not Ends

All technology transitions are cycles. Like elections. Like economic booms and busts. And in some way, the purpose is always to bring a higher level of automation, more throughput, more productivity, better quality of living.

Some waves are abruptly disruptive—like AI—affecting multiple sectors of the economy so quickly. Others are slow adoption or natural improvements where the transformation apparently only affects the tech industry initially—like virtualization—and then you slowly see the rippling effect across the rest of the economy.

10.5.2   What's Consistent: You're Never Late

Here's what matters: **you're never late**. You can always catch the next train. The next wave. Waves will always keep coming.

What's consistent across all technology transitions:

We keep building on top. Things get improved but don't get completely replaced quickly. If they do, it normally takes time. Think of fax machines—obsolete technology still used in doctors' offices when it could have been replaced 20 years ago.

I remember teaching real estate agents how to build websites 30 years ago. Still to this day, after all the apps like Zillow and Redfin, it's still a valid skill.

Humans remain in the equation. There's always expansion—more jobs, more opportunities for startups. Not elimination, but transformation and multiplication.

Problem-solving transfers. Specific technologies change. The ability to solve problems persists. That's the core skill that transferred across every wave of my career.

10.5.3   What Changes and What Stays Same

Technologies change. Tools change. Languages change. Frameworks change.

But the fundamental activities—understanding problems, designing solutions, building systems, collaborating with people—those stay constant.

Each time I adapted, I gave up something. A specific technology. A particular tool. A programming language I'd mastered.

But what stayed constant was my ability to solve problems. To learn what I needed. To adapt to new contexts.

That's the skill worth developing.

10.6   The Discomfort Decision

In 2019, I was at Deloitte in Madrid. Executive position. Amazing people. Leading a large team. Acclaimed as a leader in the industry. A key piece for closing deals. Clear career path to becoming a partner in the firm.

I was comfortable. Successful. Respected.

And I left.

Why? Because I wanted to work in research, in cutting-edge AI. I worked closely with Montse Medina and David Manzano, both PhDs in AI. I wanted to be like them. And I had a long way to go.

I wanted to return to the United States. I still wanted to learn more. I wanted to work in research, and Deloitte couldn't provide that for me at that time.

In order to do that, I had to start from square zero. Again from the bottom. Job hunting, focusing on either research-focused startups or positions where I could work in research.

This wasn't rational from a career stability perspective. I was giving up a clear path to partnership for an uncertain path to... something I wanted but hadn't yet defined clearly.

10.6.1   What Made Me Choose Discomfort

Purpose. I knew what I wanted to become, even if the path wasn't clear. I knew I wasn't satisfied with the trajectory I was on, even though it was objectively successful.

I gained a new opportunity to reinvent myself. I'm not just an engineer anymore. I'm a computer scientist in AI and machine learning.

That identity shift required leaving comfort. Required starting over. Required embracing uncertainty.

If you're not willing to be uncomfortable, you can't adapt. And if you can't adapt, you can't thrive in a world where the only constant is change.

10.7   Learning Before You Need It

One pattern that's served me well: building skills before they're immediately job-relevant.

10.7.1   What I'm Learning Now

Right now, I stay current with the latest LLM research—latest supervised learning and reinforcement learning techniques like SFT, DPO, GRPO. Not because my current role requires deep knowledge of these specific techniques, but because they inform where the field is heading.

I'm tracking agentic AI developments, robotics advances, even quantum computing—though I think the quantum technologies that will matter in 15 years don't exist today. Still, it's a long-term topic worth understanding at a foundational level.

10.7.2   How I Identify What's Worth Learning Early

This is tough. Here's my approach: check where the industry is going. Look at cutting-edge startups—what positions are they trying to fill that they can't find experts for? That tells you what skills will be valuable soon but aren't common yet.

When I learned TypeScript at Evolv, it wasn't because my immediate work required it. It was because I saw the industry shifting toward TypeScript for even standalone applications. Learning it early meant I had the skill ready when I needed it.

Same with my formal education. I started the Bachelor's degree in 2023 not because I immediately needed it, but because I knew the research path required an MS or PhD, which in turn required a BS. By the time I returned to PayPal in 2025, I had the credentials that positioned me to lead AI initiatives.

10.8 The Age Advantage

Let me address something directly: people think you get worse at learning as you age. That's wrong.

10.8.1 Why Learning at 46 Was Easier Than at 20

In my twenties, I didn't have as much purpose to learn as I have now. I thought I knew everything I needed to succeed. I was arrogant about my existing knowledge and resistant to structured learning.

Now I know what I need to learn to get where I want. That clarity makes learning faster, not slower.

I have pattern recognition built from experience. I can feel what's going to succeed and what's going to fail. I've seen it many times already. That pattern recognition helps me learn new things faster because I can connect them to existing frameworks.

10.8.2 What's Harder, What's Easier

Physically, yes, I might need more sleep than I did at 20. But intellectually? It was actually easier at 46. I had greater purpose. Better techniques. More discipline. Less ego getting in the way of learning.

The advantage of age is wisdom. Not about specific technologies—those change—but about how to learn, how to prioritize, how to connect new knowledge to existing experience.

10.8.3 The Consumer Society Trap

Here's what worries me about age and learning: it's not that brains deteriorate with age. It's that society encourages people to stop using their brains.

The consumer society we've created feeds a vicious cycle. Have kids who become consumers as early as possible. Then you can stop thinking because "it's time to rest." Entertainment becomes passive consumption rather than active engagement.

As long as you keep establishing neural connections, you'll get smarter.[38] The problem is most people, when they age, literally stop using their brain. They settle into routines. They stop learning new things. They avoid challenges.

That's a choice, not biology.

10.8.4 Advice for "I'm Too Old"

If you think you were smarter when you were younger, you're wrong. With time, you get smarter—if you keep learning.

Age is an advantage if you use it correctly. You have more context, more pattern recognition, more wisdom about what matters. Those advantages far outweigh any disadvantage in raw processing speed.

Don't let age be an excuse. Let it be an advantage.

10.9 Using AI to Accelerate Learning

Here's something new: AI tools fundamentally change how we can learn.

10.9.1 AI as Learning Partner

I use AI to create study guides and learning guides. But I make sure to use it agentically—having it obtain and search information from credible sources, not just generating plausible-sounding content.

I can use AI to explain algorithms, methods, complex papers. It's like having a tutor available 24/7 who never gets tired of explaining things different ways until you understand.

---

[38] Doidge, "The Brain That Changes Itself: Stories of Personal Triumph from the Frontiers of Brain Science", 2007.

Example: When reading dense machine learning papers, I use AI to:

- Summarize the key contributions

- Explain mathematical notation I'm unfamiliar with

- Generate examples that illustrate abstract concepts

- Connect the paper's ideas to practical applications

This dramatically accelerates the learning loop. What used to take hours of struggling with notation and abstract concepts now takes minutes with AI assistance.

10.9.2 What Still Requires Human Judgment

But here's what AI can't do: determine what's worth learning deeply versus what to skim. Decide which concepts are foundational versus which are details. Connect new learning to your specific context and goals.

That requires human judgment informed by experience and purpose.

AI is a tool that multiplies your learning capacity. But you still need to direct that capacity toward things that matter.

10.10 The Practical Learning Framework

Let me give you the actual system I use for learning something new.

10.10.1 Deep Dive Approach

When I need to learn something—a new programming language, a new ML framework, whatever—my first step is deep dive.

I find either a book, manual, or documentation. Not videos, not quick tutorials. Comprehensive resources that provide foundation.

Then I work through until I've accomplished what I originally intended. Not until I've finished the book. Until I've solved the problem or built the thing I needed to build.

This is important: **learning is not about completing resources**. It's about accomplishing goals. The resource is just the means.

How long does "enough" take? Until the goal is accomplished. Sometimes that's days. Sometimes weeks. Depends on the complexity and how well it connects to existing knowledge.

10.10.2 The 30/60/90 Day Framework

If someone wanted to adopt my learning approach, here's what I'd recommend:

First 30 days: Plan what you want to accomplish. Create a learning schedule. Start working on foundations. Don't try to learn everything—identify the core concepts that enable everything else.

By 60 days: Follow the learning schedule with no exceptions. Consistency matters more than intensity. Two hours daily beats eight hours on weekends. Build the habit of protected learning time.

By 90 days: Reflect on progress. What worked? What didn't? Can you learn better, faster, more effectively? Adjust the system based on what you've discovered about your own learning.

This framework works whether you're learning a new programming language, getting a degree, or pivoting to a new field entirely.

10.10.3 Learning Techniques That Actually Work

Based on decades of learning, here's what I know works:

Taking breaks helps retention. Your brain consolidates learning during rest. Cramming doesn't work as well as spaced repetition with breaks between sessions.

Writing helps retention massively. I learn equally well by watching or reading, but reading is simply more practical as I can go faster. And writing—whether notes, code, or explanations—helps me retain knowledge far better than passive consumption.

Building projects tests understanding. You don't know if you've learned something until you've used it to create. Theory without practice is incomplete learning.

Teaching solidifies learning. Explaining concepts to others forces you to understand them deeply. It also reveals gaps in your understanding immediately.

10.11 Why Learning Agility Matters More Now

We're living in a unique moment in history.

10.11.1 The Communication Revolution

Everyone seems to know everything now because anyone can get step-by-step guides to do anything. Anyone can ask AI to explain concepts for any type of audience.

This democratizes knowledge. But it also changes what's valuable.

Communication is king. Masters of articulation are thriving—either doing podcasts with millions of followers or getting into leadership and executive positions.

Why? Because when everyone has access to information, the value shifts to:

- Understanding what information matters

- Synthesizing information into insights

- Communicating complex ideas clearly

- Connecting ideas across domains

- Applying knowledge to novel situations

These require learning agility—the ability to quickly absorb new information, connect it to existing knowledge, and apply it effectively.

10.11.2 Why Adaptability Is THE Skill

Technology is changing faster than ever. AI is accelerating obsolescence of specific skills. The half-life of technical knowledge keeps shrinking.

In this environment, **adaptability isn't just valuable—it's the only skill that remains valuable permanently**.

You can be an expert in today's cutting-edge technology. But in five years, that expertise might be obsolete. Your ability to learn the next cutting-edge technology? That's permanent.

I've seen this again and again: specific skills became obsolete. Learning ability remained valuable. Each time I adapted, I became more valuable, not less.

10.12   Learning in Public: Writing This Book

This book itself is learning in public. That's intentional.

I'm not writing this because I have all the answers. I'm writing it because the process of explaining these ideas forces me to understand them more deeply.

Teaching through writing is learning. Articulating the pattern of adaptation across 25 years helps me see that pattern more clearly. Understanding why specific skills transfer while others don't helps me make better decisions about what to learn next.

This is learning in public: sharing your thinking as you develop it, inviting critique and discussion, refining understanding through articulation.

It's uncomfortable. You expose incomplete thoughts. You risk being wrong. But that discomfort is where learning happens.

If you want to develop learning agility, consider learning in public:

- Write about what you're learning

- Share projects as you build them

- Teach concepts as you understand them

- Invite feedback on your thinking

The visibility creates accountability. The teaching forces depth. The feedback accelerates improvement.

10.13 The Meta-Skill Advantage

Here's why learning to learn is the ultimate meta-skill:

It enables all other skills. You can't develop judgment without learning from experience. You can't cultivate creativity without learning from diverse domains. You can't build relationships without learning about people and organizations.

It compounds over time. Each thing you learn makes learning the next thing easier. You develop frameworks, patterns, techniques that accelerate future learning.

It never becomes obsolete. Programming languages change. Frameworks evolve. AI models improve. But the ability to learn new things remains valuable regardless of what changes.

It creates optionality. When you can learn quickly, you're not locked into any specific path. You can pivot. You can adapt. You can seize opportunities that others can't pursue because they lack the learning agility to make the transition.

10.14 Your Learning Journey Starts Now

I got my Bachelor's degree at 46. Master's at 48. While working full-time at demanding jobs. While building production systems. While filing patents. While writing papers.

If I can do it, you can do it.

Not necessarily degrees—those were valuable for my specific goals, but they're not the only path. What matters is committing to continuous learning, developing effective learning systems, and building the adaptability that makes you valuable regardless of technological change.

The next wave of technology is coming. You don't know what it will be. Neither do I. But I know we'll both be fine if we've developed the ability to learn whatever that wave requires.

That's the skill that survives everything. That's the skill worth investing in.

That's the skill that makes every other skill in this book possible.

The final section of this book explores what happens when you put all four skills together—judgment, creativity, connection, and learning—and use them to thrive in the AI era. Not despite AI, but because of it.

Because the future isn't about competing with AI. It's about amplifying human capabilities with AI while focusing on the work only humans can do.

And that's what we explore next.

Chapter 11

The Career Equation: Judgment × AI

11.1 What My Day Actually Looks Like

Let me show you what working with AI actually means in practice, not in theory.

11.1.1 Morning: Strategy and Coordination

I start my mornings with strategic work—the kind that requires human judgment and context.

In project team meetings, we review progress on tasks, discuss leadership direction, plan changes to existing features. These aren't status updates. They're decision-making sessions about priorities, tradeoffs, and direction.

I spend time on code reviews. Not just checking syntax, but evaluating architectural decisions, spotting patterns that will cause problems at scale, ensuring we're building maintainably.

We plan deployments. This requires understanding organizational dynamics, coordinating across teams, managing risk. When to deploy, what to deploy together, what to hold back—these are judgment calls that require context AI doesn't have.

This is human work. AI can't decide what matters strategically. It can't understand organizational politics. It can't evaluate whether code will be maintainable by the team that has to support it.

11.1.2   Midday: Collaboration and Judgment

The middle of my day focuses on human interaction—the work that creates value through relationships and shared understanding.

I have mentoring meetings with other engineers. Not teaching them syntax, but helping them navigate career decisions, develop judgment, understand organizational dynamics. The kind of learning that happens through conversation and observation, not documentation.

Sometimes pair programming. Working through a problem together, thinking out loud, sharing pattern recognition that comes from experience. This creates knowledge transfer that no documentation can capture.

And recruiting—interviewing new engineer candidates. Evaluating not just technical skills but judgment, communication, how they think about problems. Can they adapt? Do they ask good questions? Would they thrive here? These assessments require human intuition informed by years of seeing what works.

AI can't do any of this. It can't mentor. It can't build relationships. It can't evaluate cultural fit or potential for growth.

11.1.3   Afternoon: Focus Time with AI

Afternoons are my focus time—where I work by myself with AI assistance. This is where the productivity multiplication happens.

I use Claude and GitHub Copilot mainly. Claude for complex reasoning, architectural discussions, generating code for entire features. Copilot for inline suggestions, completing patterns, handling boilerplate.

I create pull requests—often substantial ones, because AI helps me build features that would have taken days in hours. And I review code from others, using AI to help spot potential issues at scale.

Here's what's changed: I can now spend 80% of my time on high-value work—deciding what to build, making architectural choices, ensuring quality—and only 20% on execution. Before AI, it was reversed: 80% execution, 20% strategic thinking.

That inversion makes me more valuable, not less.

11.2 The Math That Makes You More Valuable

People hear "AI handles 70% of execution" and think "I'm 70% less valuable."

That's backwards.

11.2.1 Why Automation Increases Your Value

Think about it this way: I have more time to work on problems that really matter, instead of wasting time executing them.

It's like having a personal assistant. Having someone handle your email, schedule meetings, and manage logistics doesn't make you less valuable. It makes you more productive by freeing you to focus on work only you can do.

AI is that assistant, but for technical execution.

Before AI, if I wanted to build a new feature, I'd spend:

- 20% of time deciding what to build and how

- 60% of time writing code

- 20% of time testing and debugging

With AI, the breakdown changes:

- 40% of time deciding what to build and how (I can explore more options)

- 20% of time directing AI to write code and reviewing output

- 40% of time on architecture, integration, and ensuring quality

Same total time. But I'm spending it on judgment, architecture, quality—the work that actually creates value. The work that requires my experience and expertise.

11.2.2 What High-Value Work Actually Means

High-value work means making decisions on what experiments are worth trying. Using experience and judgment to decide what's the right path to pursue.

It means knowing which problems matter and which are distractions. Understanding what will scale and what will break. Recognizing patterns from previous systems that predict future problems.

AI can't do this. It can execute once you've decided. But deciding what's worth executing? That requires human judgment informed by experience.

11.3 Case Study: An Admin Console

Let me show you exactly what the hybrid model looks like with a concrete example.

11.3.1 The Traditional Approach

Without AI, building an admin console would have taken approximately three months with a team of three engineers.

Those three months would have been 12 two-week sprints. Time spent on:

Sprint 1-2: Planning and work distribution. Architectural decisions. Setting up infrastructure. One engineer working on the data models. Another on API endpoints and routers. A third on initial frontend scaffolding.

Sprint 3-6: Core implementation. CRUD operations for different entities built in parallel. One engineer working on one entity while another works on a different one. Code reviews. Reconciliation when different parts need to integrate. Discussions about framework choices. Learning new libraries. Writing repetitive code that needs refactoring.

Sprint 7-9: Feature completion. Testing. Bug fixes. Integration work. Dealing with edge cases. Refactoring code that was written quickly initially.

Sprint 10-12: Polish. Performance optimization. Documentation. Deployment preparation. Final testing. Production rollout.

There's only so much that can be done at a given time with traditional development. Work gets parallelized where possible, but integration creates dependencies. Code reviews create delays. Learning curves slow progress.

11.3.2   What Actually Happened

I built it in three weeks. Just me, with AI assistance.

Week 1: Built a console that allowed testing endpoints and different models, exposing configuration options. This was the core functionality—the ability to interact with AI systems, test different configurations, see results, adjust parameters.

With AI, I could rapidly prototype different UI approaches, implement backend endpoints, create data models—all in the first week. What would have taken three engineers a month took me a week.

Week 2: Added the ability to compare models side-by-side, seeing results with different parameters simultaneously. This required more sophisticated state management, comparison logic, and UI layout. AI helped me generate the comparison components, implement the state management patterns, create the layouts.

Week 3: Finalized and deployed to production. This meant production-level error handling, logging, authentication, deployment configuration.

11.3.3   The Key Decisions I Made

AI didn't make this happen automatically. I made critical decisions that shaped the entire project:

Embedding a code editor: I decided to embed a code editor directly in the console as the primary way to tweak parameters. This was a UX decision that AI couldn't make—it required understanding how engineers work, what would feel natural, what would be efficient.

Side-by-side comparison: I decided the comparison view needed to be a first-class feature, not an afterthought. This required architectural decisions about state management and data flow.

Technology stack: I chose React for frontend and TypeScript/Node for backend because the organization already maintained libraries with custom React components. There was strong organizational support for this stack. Reinventing the wheel takes time and definitely wasn't the purpose.

These weren't technical decisions in isolation. They were organizational decisions informed by understanding the ecosystem, what would get adopted, what would be maintainable.

AI helped me quickly produce the components and screens I needed. But I decided what components to build and why.

11.3.4   The 10x Productivity Reality

Three weeks versus three months with a team of three. That's roughly 10x productivity improvement.

But it's not just speed. It's that I could iterate rapidly, try different approaches, refine the UX multiple times—all within the same timeframe that would have gotten us a basic first version with traditional development.

The quality is higher because I had more time for thoughtful architecture. The UX is better because I could experiment more. The code is cleaner because I could refactor more.

That's the multiplication effect. Not just faster execution, but better outcomes.

11.4   Case Study: The Declarative Agent Framework

The admin console was substantial, but the declarative agent framework was the kind of project that typically requires teams and months. Let me walk through how it actually happened.

11.4.1 Conceptual Design: 100% Human

The concept took two to three weeks of deep thinking. I experimented with different proposal options, trying to understand what the right abstractions should be.

This was entirely human work. AI couldn't help because the problem was: what should this system be? Not how to implement it, but what to create.

Key decisions I made during this phase:

What are the first-class components? I had to decide what the fundamental elements of the framework would be. Tools, LLMs, pipelines, functions—what abstractions would make sense for building agents? This required understanding both the technical possibilities and how engineers think about agent workflows.

Declarative nature of the language specification. I decided this should be a declarative system where you describe what you want, not an imperative system where you code how to get it. That was a fundamental architectural choice that shaped everything else.

Compiled form to produce JSON/YAML artifacts. Rather than a DSL that compiles to binary, I chose to compile to human-readable, version-controllable JSON. This tied to my insight about deployment processes—configuration deploys fast, code deploys slow.

Separation of concerns. I had to decide what parts the library handles versus what gets defined in individual services. This was about understanding business requirements, organizational structure, and technical constraints.

Tracing, audit logging, and metric collection. I decided these had to be first-class features built into the framework, not afterthoughts. This came from experience knowing that production systems without observability fail in ways you can't debug.

None of these decisions could have been made by AI. They required understanding business needs, organizational dynamics, production requirements, and having the judgment to make tradeoffs.

11.4.2   Implementation: AI-Assisted

Implementation took three to four weeks. AI assisted with creating some of the initial object abstractions, implementing functions where I didn't want to spend time on boilerplate, and giving me clues when I was stuck.

But notice what I said: AI assisted. It didn't implement. I directed, AI executed, I reviewed.

Example: I'd describe what a pipeline executor should do—take a pipeline specification, maintain state, orchestrate tools and LLMs, handle errors. AI would generate initial implementation. I'd review, identify what was missing or wrong, refine the specification, get better implementation.

This iterative process—human specification, AI implementation, human refinement—happened dozens of times. Each cycle took minutes instead of hours.

11.4.3   Testing: Heavily AI-Assisted

AI helped create unit tests entirely once I established the patterns I wanted. I'd write a few example tests showing the testing approach, then AI could generate similar tests for other components.

For functional tests, I provided the basic patterns to follow, then AI generated comprehensive test suites.

But I designed the test strategy. What needed testing? What edge cases mattered? What failure modes should we prepare for? Those were judgment calls based on experience.

11.4.4   Total Timeline and Impact

From concept to production-ready framework: roughly six to eight weeks. Just me, with AI assistance.

Without AI? This would have been a team of three to four engineers working for three to four months. Minimum. More likely six months to get to the same level of polish and completeness.

But more important than speed: the framework reduced deployment complexity from multi-team coordination to rapid iteration cycles. That impact happened because I had time to think deeply about the right abstractions, iterate on the design, build comprehensive features. AI gave me the time to do the strategic work that makes systems valuable.

11.5 Hackathon Example: Speed Changes Everything

Let me give you one more concrete example of how AI changes what's possible.

During a series of internal hackathons focused on agentic AI solutions, we had hard deadlines every two to three days. These couldn't be demos or prototypes. They had to be real, working solutions.

With AI, I was able to build working prototypes before the design team had time to work on them. I'd have a functional solution before they'd even started designing.

Then leadership would review, ask for tweaks, and I'd reimplement the final working solution—often the same day.

This wasn't just about speed. It changed the entire creative process. Instead of design → implement → test, we could do implement → design → refine. Ideas became tangible immediately, which sparked better ideas, which led to better solutions.

Before AI, hackathons meant cutting corners, building minimal prototypes, hoping leadership could imagine the final product. Now I was showing them working systems they could interact with.

That's the multiplication effect: not just faster execution, but fundamentally different workflows that produce better outcomes.

11.6 How Career Development Has Changed

The old model for career advancement is breaking down. The new model is still forming. Here's what I see happening:

11.6.1 The Old Model: Years of Grinding

Before AI, advancement was based on years of coding experience. Years of experience creating and deploying products to market. Designing, coding, architecting—doing the entire cycle repeatedly until you'd internalized the patterns.

You proved you were "ready" for senior level by being independent—solving problems and providing solutions end-to-end. The assumption was that this demonstrated accumulated experience and knowledge.

That worked when execution skill was the bottleneck. When writing code was what took time and required expertise.

11.6.2 The New Model: Judgment Under Uncertainty

Now, AI can handle execution. A junior engineer with AI assistance can produce code at a rate that would have required senior-level productivity before.

So what makes someone senior now?

Unfortunately, some managers still look at surface metrics—lines of code written, tasks created and closed. They evaluate output volume rather than outcome quality.

But the real differentiator is critical thinking and judgment. A junior with AI can feel like a senior at the surface level. They might even provide end-to-end solutions for well-defined problems.

But when you ask them to apply critical thinking—to evaluate whether this solution is the right one, to anticipate how it will fail at scale, to make tradeoffs between competing concerns—they lack the experience to know what worked and what didn't in similar situations.

How do I evaluate engineers now? It's about the critical thinking. Using their own judgment. Can they:

- Identify what problem is actually worth solving?

- Evaluate multiple approaches and choose the right one for context?

- Anticipate failure modes based on experience?

- Make tradeoffs that align with business priorities?

- Recognize when "technically correct" is organizationally wrong?

These require experience. Not years of typing code, but years of seeing what works in production, what causes outages, what gets adopted versus what gets abandoned.

11.6.3 Why Experience Matters More, Not Less

Here's the paradox: AI makes execution easier, which makes experience more valuable.

When everyone can execute quickly with AI, the differentiator becomes knowing what to execute and why. That comes from experience.[39]

My 25 years of working with complex production systems is more valuable now than before AI. Why? Because I can rapidly test ideas that would have taken weeks to prototype. I can explore architectural alternatives that would have been too expensive to try. I can build systems that incorporate lessons from decades of experience—but do it in weeks instead of months.

Fresh PhDs might have deeper theoretical knowledge. But they lack production experience. They're used to working independently in labs or building proofs of concept, disconnected from industry realities.

When we hire new PhDs, we notice they're not able to deliver as quickly as you'd expect given their theoretical knowledge. They're used to a different pace—academic research timelines, not production sprint cycles. They haven't been exposed to the constraints and chaos of real production systems at scale.

Experience with production systems—understanding what breaks under load, what customers actually need versus what they say they need, what technical debt looks like and how to avoid it—that's what makes the difference now.

---

[39] Ericsson, Krampe, and Tesch-Römer, "The Role of Deliberate Practice in the Acquisition of Expert Performance", 1993.

11.6.4   The Experienced SWE at 50 vs the Fresh PhD at 26

Both have AI tools. Both have some machine learning knowledge.

What's the experienced engineer's advantage? Years of working with complex production systems. Pattern recognition from building dozens of systems, watching some succeed and others fail. Understanding what breaks under load, what customers actually need versus what they say they need, what technical debt looks like and how to avoid it.

The fresh PhD has theoretical depth. Cutting-edge research knowledge. Deep understanding of mathematical foundations. Familiarity with the latest papers and techniques.

But in production environments, experience is decisive. The 50-year-old engineer can design systems that work at scale because they've seen what fails at scale. They can make architectural decisions quickly because they've made similar decisions before and know the consequences. They can estimate timelines accurately because they've built similar systems.

The PhD can do brilliant research. But turning research into production systems? That requires different skills—skills that come from experience, not from academic training.

This isn't about age discrimination. It's about recognizing that production engineering and academic research develop different capabilities. Both are valuable. But for building systems that scale, serve millions of users, and survive organizational change? Experience matters more than theoretical depth.

And with AI tools, that experience gap becomes even more significant. Both can execute quickly. But only the experienced engineer knows what to execute and why.

11.7   What This Means for Engineers at Different Stages

Let me be practical about what the hybrid model means for engineers at different career stages.

11.7.1 Junior Engineers (0-3 Years)

If you're early in your career, AI is both opportunity and trap.

The opportunity: You can be productive immediately. You can build features that would have required years of experience to implement. You can learn by doing rather than by studying.

The trap: If you only use AI to execute without understanding, you're not building the experience that will make you valuable. You need to understand why the code works, not just that it works.

What to focus on:

- Use AI extensively for execution, but always understand what it generates

- Build judgment by asking: "Is this the right solution, or just a working solution?"

- Seek feedback from experienced engineers on your architectural choices

- Work on problems that require creativity and judgment, not just implementation

11.7.2 Mid-Level Engineers (4-8 Years)

If you're mid-career, you have experience but might feel threatened by AI-augmented junior engineers producing at rates that previously required your level.

Your advantage: You've seen enough to have pattern recognition. You know what works and what causes problems. That judgment becomes more valuable as AI makes execution faster.

What to adapt:

- Shift from being valued for execution speed to being valued for decision quality

- Mentor junior engineers on judgment, not just code

- Take on architectural responsibilities that require experience

- Learn to use AI to multiply your impact, not just your output

11.7.3 Senior Engineers (9-15 Years)

If you're senior, you have significant experience and established reputation. But you might be comfortable with your current skills and resistant to AI tools.

Your advantage: Deep pattern recognition. Understanding of organizational dynamics. Proven track record of delivering at scale.

The risk: If you don't adopt AI tools, you'll be competing with midlevel engineers who have AI multiplication. Your experience advantage gets diluted if you're working at 1x speed while they're at 5x speed.

What to do:

- Embrace AI tools aggressively—they multiply your expertise, not replace it

- Focus on strategic work that requires your experience

- Build frameworks and systems, not just features

- Mentor others on using AI effectively with good judgment

11.7.4 Staff+ Engineers (15+ Years)

If you're at staff level or above, you might think you're most at risk—AI could potentially do much of what junior engineers do, making deep experience less valuable.

Actually, you're potentially most valuable. Here's why:

Your advantage: You have pattern recognition that spans technologies, organizations, and decades. You know what lasts and what's hype. You can design systems that survive organizational change and technology shifts.

How AI helps you:

- Test architectural ideas rapidly

- Build frameworks that enable entire organizations

- Prototype systems in days that would have taken months

- Focus entirely on strategic thinking and organizational impact

But only if you adopt AI tools. If you resist them, you become a bottleneck instead of a multiplier.

11.8   Starting Monday: The First Steps

If you're reading this and want to adopt this approach, here's exactly what to do.

11.8.1   Monday Morning: Enable the Tools

First action: Enable Copilot plugin in your IDE. This is the minimum. If you're not using at least this level of AI assistance, you're working at a disadvantage.

Not optional. Not "when I have time." Not "let me think about it." Enable it Monday morning.

11.8.2   First Week: Build Comfort

Start with small tasks. Use AI for:

- Writing boilerplate code

- Generating test cases

- Explaining code you don't understand

- Refactoring repetitive patterns

Don't try to build an entire system with AI in week one. Build comfort with the tool. Learn what it's good at and what requires human oversight.

11.8.3 First Month: Find Your Rhythm

By the end of month one, you should have a rhythm:

- Strategic thinking and architecture decisions: entirely human

- Implementation and boilerplate: heavily AI-assisted

- Review and quality assurance: human with AI helping to spot issues

- Collaboration and mentorship: entirely human

Track your time. Where are you spending effort? Where is AI saving you time? Where do you still need to do things manually?

11.8.4 First Quarter: Measure Impact

By three months, you should see measurable differences:

- Features that used to take weeks now take days

- You have more time for strategic thinking and architecture

- Code quality is higher because you can iterate more

- You're taking on more ambitious projects because execution isn't the bottleneck

If you're not seeing this, you're either not using AI effectively or you're using it for the wrong things.

11.9 The Reality: Supervision Required

Let me be honest about the challenges.

11.9.1 AI Isn't Autonomous

I use AI for everything in my work. But everything needs supervision.

AI can generate entire features. But I review every line. I verify architectural decisions. I check that it understood the business requirements correctly. I ensure it's not creating technical debt or security issues.

The supervision is quick—much faster than writing the code myself. But it's not optional.

11.9.2   The Rabbit Hole Problem

One thing that's harder than expected: it's easy to get into rabbit holes with AI.

You ask it to generate something. The output is 80% right but 20% wrong. You point out the errors. It generates new code that fixes those issues but introduces different problems. You iterate. Suddenly you've spent an hour refining something that would have taken 30 minutes to write yourself.

Learning to recognize when you're in a rabbit hole—when it's faster to just write the code yourself—is a skill you develop with experience.

11.9.3   Percentage of AI-Generated Code

People ask what percentage of my code is AI-generated versus handwritten. Honestly, it's hard to say these days.

For boilerplate and standard patterns: probably 90% AI-generated with human review.

For complex logic and architecture: maybe 50% AI-generated, 50% human-written, 100% human-reviewed.

For critical systems and security-sensitive code: AI helps with implementation, but I'm writing the core logic and reviewing everything carefully.

The question itself is somewhat wrong though. It's not about percentage of code. It's about allocation of human time. I spend my time on judgment and architecture. AI handles execution. That division of labor is what matters.

11.10   Why This Model Works

The hybrid model—human judgment plus AI execution—works because it aligns with how value is actually created in engineering.

11.10.1   Value Comes from Decisions, Not Typing

The value I create isn't in the code I type. It's in:

- Deciding which problems are worth solving

- Choosing architectures that will scale and be maintainable

- Making tradeoffs that align with business priorities

- Designing systems that others can build on

- Preventing mistakes that would cause outages or security issues

AI can't do any of that. But it can handle the mechanical work of translating those decisions into working code.

11.10.2   Experience Compounds With AI

My 25 years of experience becomes more valuable when combined with AI tools, not less. Because I can test more ideas, iterate faster, build more ambitious systems.

A junior engineer with AI can build what I specify. But they can't specify what to build. That requires experience they don't have yet.

11.10.3   The Multiplication Is Real

I'm genuinely 10x more productive than I was three years ago. Not in lines of code written—that's the wrong metric. But in impact created, systems deployed, problems solved.

That multiplication makes me more valuable to the organization, not less. Because the bottleneck was never my ability to type code. It was my time to think strategically, make decisions, and ensure quality.

AI removed the execution bottleneck. That freed me to focus on the strategic work that actually creates value.

11.11   The New Career Equation

Here's what it comes down to:

In the old model, your value was: *Years of Experience × Execution Speed*

In the new model, your value is: *Quality of Judgment × AI Multiplication Factor*

The multiplication factor is roughly the same for everyone who adopts AI tools. So the differentiator is judgment quality.

And judgment quality comes from experience—not years of typing code, but years of seeing what works in production, what fails at scale, what gets adopted versus abandoned.

That's why the hybrid model works: AI multiplies the value of human judgment. The better your judgment, the more valuable AI makes you.

The engineers who thrive will be those who:

- Develop excellent judgment through experience

- Learn to use AI tools effectively

- Focus on strategic work that requires human context

- Continuously adapt as AI capabilities evolve

The engineers who struggle will be those who:

- Resist AI tools and try to compete on execution speed

- Focus on typing code rather than making decisions

- Don't develop judgment beyond following patterns

- Assume their current skills will always be valuable

The choice is yours. But the equation is clear: in the AI era, judgment multiplied by AI execution creates value that neither alone can match.

The next chapter explores what happens when you put all four skills together—judgment, creativity, connection, and learning—and deliberately build a career that's not just AI-resistant, but AI-amplified.

Because that's the real opportunity: not competing with AI, but becoming irreplaceable by combining AI capabilities with uniquely human skills.

Chapter 12

Building Your "Automation-Proof" Career

12.1 The Honest Truth About Safety

Let me be clear. Nothing is truly automation-proof. That's a lie people tell themselves for comfort.

What exists instead: paths that are much safer than others. Strategies that position you where humans remain essential. Ways of working that make you more valuable as AI improves, not less.

But there are no guarantees. Technology keeps changing. Markets shift. Companies fail. Even the best positioning can't protect you from everything.

What you can do: understand the pattern, position yourself deliberately, build skills that compound, and stay adaptable enough to shift when the next wave arrives.

That's not a guarantee. It's a strategy. And it's worked for me across four waves of supposed obsolescence.

Let me show you how.

12.2 The Four-Category Audit

Here's how I evaluate whether it's time to make a change. Four questions, scored intuitively:

Productivity: Is my work actually providing value to the company?

Not "am I busy," but "does what I'm building matter?"

Judgment: Am I bringing my own judgment to decisions, or am I just executing what someone else decided?

Relationships: Are my professional relationships enriching me, or am I always the one giving without receiving?

Creativity: Can I use my creativity? Do I have the freedom to implement creative solutions, or am I constrained to follow established patterns?

When all four score poorly, it's time to move. When three score poorly, I start planning the transition. When two score poorly, I'm actively looking for opportunities to shift.

This isn't scientific. It's intuitive evaluation based on how I feel about my work, what I'm learning, and whether I'm growing.

12.2.1 What "Scoring Poorly" Actually Looks Like

Let me give you concrete examples.

Productivity scoring poorly: At one point in my career, I was asked to implement a complex caching layer prematurely. The real problem was a network issue that needed investigation and fixing. But leadership wanted the caching layer because it felt like "doing something." I knew this wouldn't solve the actual problem. I built it anyway. That's when I knew my productivity was being wasted on work that didn't provide real value.

Judgment scoring poorly: When you're just implementing what someone else decided without bringing your own judgment to the problem. When you're a puppet executing instructions rather than an engineer solving problems. I felt this during phases where I was being micromanaged to do things that didn't make sense—asked to add unnecessary complexity instead of finding root causes.

Relationships scoring poorly: When you're always the one helping others but when you need help or support, it's not reciprocated. Or worse, when the environment becomes what I call a "kindergarten playground"—everyone blaming everyone else, politics over substance, personal conflicts over professional goals. I've seen this at several startups. In those environments, if you focus on goals and what really matters rather than participating in the blame game, you position yourself as a leader. But if the entire culture is toxic, no amount of personal integrity fixes it. Time to leave.

Creativity scoring poorly: When you want to implement a creative solution but are told to just do it the standard way. When there's no room for innovation, no appetite for trying different approaches, no freedom to experiment. This is death for someone like me who thrives on solving problems creatively.

12.2.2   The Signal: When Work Becomes Too Easy

There's one clear signal I've learned to recognize: when I feel that I'm being asked to do work that's very easy for me, not challenging, repetitive, or that I'm not learning at all.

That's when it's time to move on.

I analyze the options and figure out what I'd be doing if I continued at the same company for one more year. That projection tells me whether to stay or go.

Some people evaluate differently. They look at safety, income, career advancement within the organization. That's the Deloitte path—Junior Engineers (Consultants) work 20 years at the firm and become Partners.

This is not how I look at career advancement. To me, the career goal is to be able to contribute to humanity's knowledge.

Different people optimize for different things. You need to know what you're optimizing for.

12.3   The Three Zones: Where You Are and Where You're Going

Think of your career as existing in three zones:

Zone 1: The Danger Zone

- Purely execution-based work

- Repetitive cognitive tasks

- Minimal judgment required

- Little human interaction needed

- Examples: Data entry, routine coding, basic analysis

AI will increasingly handle this work. If you're primarily in Zone 1, you're at high risk.

Zone 2: The Transition Zone

- Mix of execution and judgment

- Increasingly AI-assisted

- Value shifting toward oversight

- Examples: Software engineering, design, content creation

This is where most knowledge workers are right now. The work isn't disappearing, but it's transforming rapidly. You need to be actively moving toward Zone 3.

Zone 3: The Safe Zone

- High judgment, low repeatability

- Relationship-dependent

- Creative and strategic

- Context and culture-heavy

- Examples: Leadership, strategy, innovation, complex problem-solving

This is where humans remain essential. Not because AI can't do the tasks, but because the work requires context, relationships, and judgment that AI fundamentally lacks.

12.3.1 My Journey Through the Zones

Let me show you my actual progression with specific percentages:

Early career (2001-2016): 90% Execution, 10% Strategy

At Sausage Software, Use Labs, Crunchyroll—I was primarily executing. Writing code. Building products. Following specifications. Making technical decisions within constrained scope. Very fast, very productive, very replaceable.

My value was entirely based on execution speed. I could build things quickly. That was enough then.

Mid-career (2016-2019): 60% Execution, 40% Architecture/Design

At Jetlore/PayPal, I moved into more architecture and design work. Leading integration efforts. Making technical decisions with broader scope. But still spending significant time on implementation—actually writing the code, debugging issues, optimizing performance.

This is when I realized the credential gap. I could do strategic ML work, but I couldn't access the roles I wanted without formal degrees.

Transition period (2019-2022): Deliberate Repositioning, 40% Execution, 60% Strategy/Leadership

RetailNext, Clovers, back to Deloitte briefly. Each role was chosen to build specific capabilities while reducing execution percentage.

At RetailNext, after negotiating my way onto the CV team, I spent less time on implementation and more on architecture and research. This was deliberate—I was positioning myself for research roles.

Recent (2022-2024): 30% Execution, 70% Strategy/Research

At Evolv AI, I was doing research and development. Designing generative AI systems. Making strategic decisions about algorithms and architectures. Still implementing—someone has to write the code—but the execution served strategic goals I was defining.

Current (2025-present): 20% Execution, 80% High-Value Work

At my current role, about 20% of my time is execution—writing code, implementing features, building prototypes. But it's strategic execution.

189

Frameworks that enable others. Infrastructure that multiplies team effectiveness.

The 80%? Strategic planning in morning meetings. Code review providing architectural feedback. Mentoring engineers. Recruiting. Making decisions about what to build and why. Building consensus among executives. Defining technical direction.

This is firmly Zone 3 work. High judgment, relationship-dependent, strategic.

12.3.2 How I Built This Transition

Did I build this deliberately or did it happen organically?

Both. The overall trajectory was deliberate—I knew I wanted to move toward research and strategic work. But the specific steps were opportunistic, taking advantage of circumstances while steering toward the goal.

Looking back, what could I have done faster? Started the degrees earlier. Built public visibility sooner. Been more deliberate about documenting my innovations.

What would I tell my younger self? Don't wait to feel "ready" before pursuing what you want. The credentials matter—get them. The visibility matters—build it. The relationships matter—invest in them. Time compounds everything. Start early.

12.4 The Deloitte Decision Revisited

November 2019. I was a Principal at Deloitte in Madrid. Leading a team of 10. Executive position. Clear path to partnership.

The four-category audit:

Productivity: The work was valuable to Deloitte, but was it contributing to humanity's knowledge? Was I advancing the field or building client deliverables?

Judgment: I made decisions within consulting constraints. But I wanted to make research decisions—what to investigate, what to discover, what to publish.

Relationships: I worked with brilliant people like Montse Medina and David Manzano, both PhDs in AI. But I wasn't their peer academically. I wanted to work at their level, not adjacent to it.

Creativity: Consulting has constraints. Client budgets. Established methodologies. I wanted freedom to pursue ideas that might fail, to innovate without needing client approval.

Three of four categories were misaligned with my goals. Time to move.

I left my Principal position to become a Senior SWE at RetailNext. Giving up executive title, partnership track, comfortable salary.

For what? The ability to work on computer vision. Access to the US AI ecosystem. Time to pursue my degrees.

On paper: career suicide. In reality: strategic repositioning for where I wanted to go.

12.5 The RetailNext Campaign: A Case Study in Repositioning

Let me show you exactly how deliberate repositioning works.

12.5.1 The Setup

I joined RetailNext as Senior Software Engineer doing cloud engineering. Multi-cloud deployment, Cassandra databases, infrastructure work.

Not what I wanted. But it got me in the door. Got me back to Silicon Valley. Gave me stable income while pursuing my Bachelor's degree.

From day one, I knew: this role is temporary. Computer vision is the target.

12.5.2 The Year-Long Strategy

I learned from my mistake at PayPal after the Jetlore acquisition. There, I'd tried to force a transition by criticizing management, complaining about the credential gap, pushing for immediate role change.

It backfired. One thing I learned: never criticize or complain about poor management, poor leadership, never be harsh on anyone even if you're right. This never sits well.

At RetailNext, different approach:

First: Excel at current role. I did excellent cloud engineering work. Delivered what I was hired to do. Built trust. Established credibility.

Second: Build relationships with target team. Casual conversations with the computer vision team. Showing genuine interest in their work. Helping with problems when asked. Not pushing, not demanding. Just being present and useful.

Third: Go around formal hierarchy. The Director and CTO didn't see the need to move me to CV. That position was filled. It wasn't a priority for leadership. I was more valuable doing cloud engineering that nobody else could do.

So I went to the CV team manager directly. After a year of relationship-building. Offered to split my time 50/50 between cloud and CV work.

He said yes because he'd seen me work, knew I could contribute, and trusted I'd deliver.

12.5.3   The Timeline

Year 1: Cloud engineering full-time while building CV relationships.

Year 1 + 2 months: 50/50 split, proving I could deliver on CV work.

Year 1 + 4 months onward: Full transition to computer vision team.

Total time from joining RetailNext to working on what I actually wanted: 16 months.

This felt slow at the time. In retrospect, it was fast. A year of patient relationship-building enabled a transition that formal processes would have blocked.

12.6 Building Visible Expertise

The outline talks about why being "good at your job" isn't enough. Let me explain what I learned about this.

12.6.1 The Patent Strategy

I have various provisional patents. Two on AI-powered women's health management using biosensor earrings. One on the declarative commerce agent framework.

Were these deliberate career positioning? Yes and no.

The patents emerged organically from work I was doing. I wasn't inventing things to get patents. I was solving problems, and the solutions turned out to be patent-worthy.

But filing them was deliberate strategy. I could have built the same systems without filing patents. The patents don't protect much— provisional patents especially. But they create visible proof of innovation.

When someone looks at my resume, the patents signal: this person creates novel solutions, thinks about intellectual property, operates at a level where innovation matters.

12.6.2 The Patent Process Reality

The actual innovation is where the work is. Conceiving the approach, designing the system, making it work. That's all me.

The patent process is back and forth with lawyers. They handle mostly everything—prior art searches, claim drafting, formal language. You explain your innovation, answer their questions, review drafts.

It's tedious but not difficult. And worth doing for the credibility signal.

12.6.3 Have Patents Opened Doors?

I haven't fully experienced that yet. The patents are recent—filed in 2024 and 2025.

But I expect they give credibility. This is how I see it when I look at somebody else's CV. Three patents signals: this person innovates at a level worth protecting legally. That matters when evaluating candidates for strategic roles.

12.6.4 This Book as Visible Expertise

Writing this book is learning in public. That's intentional.

I'm not writing because I have all the answers. I'm writing to:

- Solidify my own understanding of the patterns I've lived through

- Build reputation as someone who thinks deeply about AI and career adaptation

- Create visible artifact that demonstrates I can communicate complex ideas clearly

- Position myself for academic research and teaching roles

This is strategic. Public visibility compounds over time. A book is permanent visible expertise that continues working for you years after publication.

12.6.5 Building Visibility Without Patents or Books

What if you don't have patents? What if writing a book isn't realistic?

Other options that work:

- Internal presentations that get you known within your organization

- Blog posts that demonstrate your thinking (even if nobody reads them at first)

- Contributing to open source projects that matter in your field

- Teaching what you're learning through documentation or mentorship

- Speaking at meetups or local conferences

- Building side projects that showcase your capabilities

What matters isn't the medium. It's consistent demonstration of expertise in areas you want to be known for.

Start small. Build consistently. Let it compound over years.

12.7 The Skills Portfolio: What I Actually Built

The outline distinguishes "must-haves" from "differentiators." Let me show you mine.

12.7.1 The Must-Haves (Table Stakes)

AI Tool Fluency:

I use Claude and GitHub Copilot extensively. Started experimenting with GPT-3 in 2020 when most people thought it was just a toy. By the time GPT-4 arrived, I had three years of experience working with LLMs.

That early adoption gave me pattern recognition others lack. I know what LLMs are good at, what they struggle with, how to prompt effectively, when to use them versus when to code myself.

This is table stakes now. If you're not fluent with AI tools, you're working at a disadvantage. Not optional.

Clear Communication:

This took work. English isn't my first language. I'm from Barcelona, moved to the US in my twenties. I had to deliberately improve my technical communication—writing papers, presenting to executives, explaining complex ideas simply.

Why is this must-have now? Because when everyone has access to AI tools for execution, the differentiator is explaining what to build and why. Communication becomes the bottleneck.

Business Acumen:

Understanding organizational dynamics. What actually gets adopted versus what gets abandoned. How decisions really get made versus what the org chart suggests.

I learned this through mistakes. Criticizing management and watching it backfire. Seeing what works at different companies. Learning from mentors like my former CTO who taught me about relationship capital.

This develops through experience and observation. Pay attention to how decisions get made. Learn the unwritten rules. Understand what leadership actually cares about.

12.7.2 My Differentiators (The 2-3 That Created Advantage)

Deep Domain Expertise in AI Infrastructure:

I didn't just use AI tools. I built frameworks for deploying AI at scale. That specialization came from deliberate focus in my recent roles.

This emerged partly from timing—I was positioned in AI infrastructure during the GenAI boom—but I made it deliberate by going deep rather than staying surface-level.

Cross-Functional Bridge (Tech + Business):

I can speak both technical and business languages. Engineers trust me because I can code. Executives trust me because I understand business priorities. Product managers trust me because I care about users.

This capability came from working across different roles and companies. From startups where you do everything to enterprises where you specialize. From technical roles to leadership roles.

I wish I'd developed this earlier. Understanding business priorities accelerates everything—you stop building technically impressive things nobody needs and start building things that create business value.

Innovation Track Record:

Three patents. Academic paper. Multiple frameworks deployed at scale. This wasn't accidental.

I deliberately pursued patent-worthy innovations. Not for money—provisional patents don't pay. For credibility. For positioning myself as someone who innovates, not just executes.

12.7.3 How to Choose Your Differentiators

Don't pick randomly. Look at:

What you're naturally drawn to. I'm drawn to building frameworks and infrastructure. That became my differentiator because I enjoyed it enough to go deep.

What the market needs. AI infrastructure engineers are in high demand. If I'd specialized in something with no market demand, the expertise wouldn't matter.

What compounds over time. Framework-building compounds—each framework teaches you patterns that make the next one easier. Leadership compounds—each person you mentor potentially helps you later.

Pick 2-3 areas where your natural interests align with market demand and where expertise compounds over years.

12.8 The Practical 90-Day Repositioning Plan

The outline suggests this. Let me tell you what this actually looked like for me—not as formal sprint, but as pattern I've repeated.

12.8.1 Month 1: Automate and Audit

Week 1-2: Automate Your Routine Work

Use AI tools aggressively. Free up 5-10 hours per week by automating execution work.

I did this at PayPal immediately. Tasks that used to take me hours—generating boilerplate, writing tests, creating documentation—now take minutes with AI assistance.

That freed time doesn't disappear. It gets reallocated to strategic work.

Week 3-4: Audit Where Time Goes

Track your time for two weeks. Categorize everything as execution, strategic, meetings, learning.

When I did this informally at various points, I discovered I was being asked to do work that was too easy, that wasn't challenging, that I wasn't learning from.

That realization drove transitions. If you're not learning, you're not growing. If you're not growing, you're becoming obsolete.

12.8.2 Month 2: Take On One Strategic Project

This is where deliberate repositioning happens.

At RetailNext, my strategic project was: get onto the computer vision team. That took a year, but I started month one.

At my current company, my strategic project was: build a declarative agent framework that the organization needed. That became my primary focus and established me as a strategic thinker.

The project should:

- Require judgment and experience, not just execution

- Create value beyond your immediate team

- Position you as strategic contributor

- Be visible to leadership

You might need to do this outside work hours initially. But freed-up time from AI automation makes this possible.

12.8.3 Month 3: Build One Strategic Relationship

Identify one person who's doing work you want to do or who can help you get there.

At RetailNext, this was the Computer Vision team manager I spent a year building relationship with. Not transactional—genuine interest in his work, offering help when possible, being patient.

At a major fintech company, this was executives I presented the declarative agent framework concept to early. Building shared understanding before I needed approval.

The relationship needs to be genuine. People sense when you're just networking for advantage. But when you're genuinely interested in their work and can contribute value, relationships develop naturally.

12.9 The 2-Year Career Evolution

If you execute the 90-day cycle consistently, here's what changes over two years:

12.9.1 Year 1: Foundation and Momentum

Quarter 1: Automate execution work. Take on one strategic project. Build one key relationship. These feel small initially.

Quarter 2: Freed-up time enables more strategic work. Deliver visible results from strategic project. Expand network based on initial relationship.

Quarter 3: Propose larger initiative based on Q1-Q2 success. Demonstrate strategic thinking publicly. Mentor others, which positions you as experienced contributor.

Quarter 4: Position yourself for promotion or role expansion. Or start planning transition to new company if current organization doesn't provide growth path.

This was roughly my path from 2023-2024: automated heavily with AI tools, built the foundation for agentic AI frameworks at Evolv AI, completed Bachelor's degree, positioned for return to PayPal.

12.9.2 Year 2: Establishment and Impact

Quarter 1: New role or expanded scope. I returned with a mandate to build agentic AI capabilities from the ground up.

Quarter 2: Establish yourself in strategic position. I delivered the declarative agent framework, which gained adoption across multiple teams.

Quarter 3: Build visible expertise. I wrote an academic paper and continued building my patent portfolio.

Quarter 4: Firmly established in Zone 3. Creating opportunities for others. I'm now mentoring engineers on AI, contributing to technical direction, enabling teams.

Two years of deliberate action transformed trajectory from execution-focused to strategy-focused career.

12.10   What Doesn't Work: Lessons From Mistakes

Let me be honest about failures and mistakes in repositioning.

12.10.1   The Criticism Mistake

After Jetlore acquisition in 2016-2019, I wanted to move to ML teams. The credential gap was blocking me. I was frustrated.

I criticized management about the credential requirement. I complained about decisions. I was harsh about what I perceived as unfairness.

It didn't work. It positioned me as difficult, as someone who fights against organizational reality rather than working within it.

What I should have done: recognized the credential gap and started building credentials immediately. Worked within the system while preparing to change the system.

I learned: never criticize leadership publicly, even when you're right. Focus on what you can control—your own skills, your own positioning. Not what you can't control—organizational policies, hiring requirements.

12.10.2   Staying Too Long in Comfortable Roles

At several companies, I stayed longer than I should have because it was comfortable. Good salary. Interesting enough work. Decent people.

But I wasn't growing. Wasn't learning at the rate I needed. Wasn't positioning for the future.

The mistake: optimizing for short-term comfort over long-term growth.

What I learned: when work becomes too easy, it's time to move. Comfort is dangerous. Challenge drives growth.

12.10.3 Not Building Public Visibility Sooner

I should have been writing blog posts in 2015. Giving talks in 2018. Building public portfolio earlier.

I waited until I felt "credible enough." That was a mistake. You build credibility by sharing ideas publicly, not by waiting until you already have credibility.

This book is partly correcting that mistake. But I've lost years of compounding visibility.

Start building public expertise early, even if you feel like you don't know enough yet. The act of explaining publicly forces you to deepen your understanding.

12.11 The Timeline Question: How Long Does This Take?

People want to know: how long until I'm "safe"?

12.11.1 Realistic Expectations

From recognizing you need to reposition to being established in Zone 3: 2-5 years typically.

My path:

- 2019: Recognized credential gap and need to reposition

- 2019-2023: Built credentials (degrees), capabilities (diverse roles), visible expertise (starting patents process)

- 2024-2025: Bootstrapped agentic AI, firmly in Zone 3

Six years total. Could it have been faster? Maybe 4 years if I'd been more aggressive. But trying to rush credentialing while working full-time has limits.

12.11.2 For People Starting Now

If you're in Zone 2 right now and want to move to Zone 3:

Have strong foundation already? 1-2 years possible. Focus on strategic projects, build visible expertise, leverage existing relationships.

Need significant repositioning? 3-4 years realistic. Need to build new capabilities, possibly get credentials, establish track record.

Major career change? 4-5 years. Changing industries or domains while building expertise takes time.

But here's the key: time passes anyway. You can spend 4 years staying in the same place, or 4 years deliberately repositioning. Either way, it's 4 years.

12.12 For Different Starting Points

Let me give specific advice based on where you are now.

12.12.1 Early Career (Danger Zone)

If you're doing primarily execution work, you're vulnerable. But you have time.

Immediate actions:

- Learn AI tools extensively—Copilot minimum, Claude/ChatGPT for complex work

- Volunteer for ambiguous projects that require judgment

- Build relationships with experienced engineers you can learn from

- Start building public visibility (write, contribute to open source, teach)

Two-year goal: Shift from pure execution to execution + judgment. Position yourself as someone who makes good decisions, not just someone who implements quickly.

12.12.2 Mid-Career Feeling Stuck

If you're 10-15 years in and feeling threatened by AI-augmented juniors:

Your advantage: Experience and pattern recognition. You've seen what fails. You know what scales. That's more valuable now, not less.

Your risk: If you're competing on execution speed, you'll lose. AI multiplies junior engineers' execution to levels that match yours.

What to do:

- Embrace AI tools immediately—multiply your own execution

- Shift explicitly toward strategic and architectural work

- Mentor juniors on judgment—this positions you as experienced leader

- Document your decision-making process—this builds visible expertise

Two-year goal: Move from "experienced executor" to "strategic architect." Your value is judgment and experience, not typing speed.

12.12.3 Senior But Not Strategic

If you're senior in title but not doing strategic work:

You're at risk despite seniority. Title doesn't protect you. Type of work does.

Immediate actions:

- Audit your actual work—how much is execution versus strategy?

- Identify what strategic work exists in your organization

- Volunteer for it or propose creating it

- Build relationships with executives making strategic decisions

- Consider whether current organization allows strategic growth or if you need to move

I was in this position at RetailNext doing cloud engineering. I had to actively campaign for CV role. Took a year. But it positioned me for everything that followed.

12.12.4   The Urgent Case: Pure Execution Role

If you're in pure execution role that's clearly being automated:

This is urgent. Don't wait. Don't hope it works out. Act now.
Immediate steps:

1. Enable AI tools today. Not Monday. Today.

2. Free up time by automating everything you can

3. Use freed time to learn strategic skills

4. Start job searching for roles with more judgment/strategy component

5. Build credentials if you lack them (certifications, degrees, visible projects)

Timeline: 6-12 months to make meaningful transition. This requires aggressive action.

The longer you wait, the harder it gets. Market moves fast. People who reposition early have advantage.

12.13   Do I Feel Secure?

The outline asks if I feel "automation-proof." Let me be honest.

12.13.1 What Makes Me Confident

I feel secure not because I'm immune to automation, but because I've positioned myself where I'm valuable regardless of how AI evolves:

I build AI infrastructure. Someone has to create the frameworks that let AI work at enterprise scale. That's not getting automated soon.

I have proven track record. Patents, papers, frameworks deployed. Visible expertise that's documented and recognized.

I can adapt quickly. I've done it four times. I know the pattern. When the next wave arrives, I'll adapt again.

I have optionality. If the company disappears, I could get hired elsewhere. My skills are in demand. My network is strong.

12.13.2 What Still Concerns Me

But I'm not complacent. What worries me:

The rate of change is accelerating. Each wave happens faster than the last. The next wave might require adaptation faster than I'm used to.

Age discrimination is real. At 48, I'm older than most people in tech. Some companies won't hire people my age regardless of capability.

Credentials might not be enough. I have BS and MS now. But if everyone gets degrees and the bar keeps rising, I might need PhD eventually. That's 4-5 more years while working.

12.13.3 What I'm Doing to Stay Ahead

I'm not waiting to see what happens. I'm positioning proactively:

Building public visibility through this book. Creating permanent artifact that demonstrates expertise.

Staying current with latest AI research. Reading papers weekly. Experimenting with new models and techniques before they're mainstream.

Considering PhD path. Not immediately, but as potential next step. Contributing to academic research requires academic credentials at highest level.

Maintaining broad network. Relationships across companies. People who've gone to different places. Optionality if I need to move.

Security comes from continuous positioning, not from having arrived somewhere safe.

12.14   Your Action Plan Starting Monday

Here's exactly what to do:

Monday: Four-category audit. Score honestly. Understand where you are.

This Week: Enable AI tools. Copilot at absolute minimum. Start automating routine work.

This Month: Identify one strategic project. Something requiring judgment. Propose it or volunteer for it.

This Quarter: Execute first 90-day cycle. Automate, strategic project, one key relationship.

This Year: Repeat cycle four times. Measurably shift time allocation from execution to strategy.

Next Two Years: Continue cycles. Build visible expertise. Get credentials if needed. Position deliberately.

This isn't guarantee. But it's strategy that's worked across 25 years and four technology waves.

The work is transforming. Those who position deliberately will thrive. Those who wait and hope will struggle.

The evidence is clear. The question is: will you act on it?

But there's a deeper question we haven't addressed yet. We've talked about skills, careers, positioning. All of it assumes we know what we're optimizing for.

What if we're asking the wrong question entirely?

That's what comes next.

Chapter 13

What If We're Asking the Wrong Question?

13.1 The Education Paradox

Let me start with the obvious question: what should we teach our kids?

The world is changing faster than education systems can adapt. Schools teach skills that AI will master. Degrees take four years while AI evolves in months. We're preparing students for jobs that don't exist yet using methods designed for jobs that no longer exist.

So what matters?

13.1.1 The Foundation That Transfers

I'm teaching my mentees—and this is what I'd teach my own kids—that foundations matter more than specifics.

Not "learn Python" but "understand how to think about computation." Not "master this framework" but "develop the ability to learn any framework quickly." Not "memorize algorithms" but "understand the principles that make algorithms work."

The meta-skills:

- Learning techniques that work regardless of subject

- Communication skills that transfer across contexts

- Systems thinking that applies to any complex domain

- Adaptability as a practiced capability

The more general knowledge exposure they have, the better. Breadth creates connection points. Depth in one narrow area is fragile when that area becomes obsolete.

13.1.2 The Coding Question

This might seem counterintuitive, but I actually think it's more important than ever to master coding. At a higher level of abstraction, yes, but understanding code matters.

Think about it this way: a software engineer uses Copilot the same way an accountant uses a calculator. The tool handles execution, but understanding what the tool is doing enables judgment about whether the output is correct.

Education programs need to adapt the same way calculators became allowed in STEM programs. Not "students must write code by hand to prove understanding," but "students must understand code well enough to judge AI-generated solutions."

13.1.3 The 2040 Vision

Here's what I envision for software engineering by 2040:

Code will be transpiled to any programming language at runtime, from highly detailed "vibe coding"—natural language specifications with intent—down to near machine code, depending on platform and performance requirements.

Core skills that remain relevant:

- Systems thinking and architecture design

- Understanding computational complexity and tradeoffs

- Debugging and problem decomposition

- Security and safety principles (probably even more relevant)

Emerging skills that will matter most:

- **Specification Engineering:** Precisely conveying intent to AI systems through structured natural language

- **Verification & Validation:** Ensuring AI-generated code meets requirements and safety constraints

- **AI Collaboration:** Working symbiotically with AI agents, knowing when to guide versus delegate

- **Domain Modeling:** Creating formal representations that bridge human understanding and machine execution

- **Ethical Engineering:** Embedding fairness, privacy, and human values into automated systems

The engineers who thrive will operate at the intersection of human intent and machine capability. Orchestrating AI systems rather than writing code directly. Moving from "how to implement" to "what should exist and why."

13.1.4 What My Degrees Actually Taught Me

I finished my Bachelor's in 2024 at 46. Master's in 2025 at 48. Both from Western Governors University, with additional graduate coursework at UT Austin.

What was valuable? The systematic way they taught me to review dozens of papers in NLP, neural networks, computer vision, deep learning. The depth of understanding in foundational concepts. The rigor of explaining complex topics clearly.

What was outdated? I remember taking algorithms courses 25 years ago where the curriculum was already 20 years outdated. That's still true. Some course content felt disconnected from industry practice.

What frustrated me: even though programs try, BS and MS programs aren't completely industry-oriented. For my personal opinion, I wish both BS and MS could have two tracks: industry and research.

But overall, the experience was meaningful. Learning in depth rather than breadth. Developing systematic approaches to understanding new domains. That's valuable regardless of specific content.

13.2   But Here's What I'm Really Asking

Skills matter. Education matters. Preparing for the future matters.

But I think we're asking the wrong question.

The question everyone asks: "What skills will survive AI?"

The better question: "What makes work meaningful beyond economic productivity?"

Because here's the thing: if AI can handle 90% of execution tasks, we're not facing unemployment. We're facing a choice about what to do with time that's no longer required for survival.

That's not a crisis. That's an opportunity.

Let me explain what I mean by telling you something personal.

13.3   The Path I Didn't Take

Spain, 1999. I was 22 years old, starting mathematics coursework at Universitat Autònoma de Barcelona.

I loved it. The rigor. The abstraction. The pursuit of understanding for its own sake. This is what I wanted to do with my life—pure research, contributing to mathematical and computational knowledge.

Then I read the cover of a book: *"Investigar en España es llorar"* ("To do research in Spain is to cry").

I understood immediately. The economic and systemic barriers ahead. The funding constraints. The limited opportunities for research careers. The reality that pursuing pure research in Spain would mean decades of struggle with no guarantee of success.

I had to find other ways forward.

At 22, I came to the United States. Not to pursue research—I lacked the credentials, the connections, the resources. To build a career in software engineering. It was not my first choice. It was the viable one.

For nearly two decades, I channeled my intellectual curiosity into building production systems, developing novel algorithms, solving real-world technical challenges. Always with the knowledge that formal research remained out of reach without the credentials I lacked.

But the desire to contribute to fundamental research never disappeared.

13.3.1 The Long Road Back

At 46, I started my Bachelor's degree. At 48, I finished my Master's. At 48, I'm writing academic papers, filing patents, positioning myself for the research work I wanted to do at 22.

It took 26 years to get back to where I wanted to go.

Was it wasted time? No. The industry experience gives me perspective that pure researchers lack. I understand how to build systems that work at scale, how to translate theory into practice, how to solve real problems with constraints.

But it wasn't the direct path. It was the necessary detour.

13.3.2 What This Taught Me About Work

Here's what those 26 years revealed: **the work that matters most to you is the work you'd do regardless of economic necessity.**

I built production systems for money. I enjoyed it, learned from it, got good at it. But it wasn't my purpose.

My purpose was always research. Understanding for its own sake. Contributing to humanity's knowledge. Creating theories and systems that advance the field.

That's what I'm finally able to do now. Not because I'm wealthy enough to ignore money—I'm not. But because I've positioned myself where my purpose and my work align.

13.4   What I Actually Value in My Work

Let me be vulnerable about something.

I don't value lines of code written. I don't particularly care about GitHub commits or tasks completed. Those are metrics that measure activity, not meaning.

Salary and status matter—I'm not pretending they don't. But they're instrumental. Means to an end. The salary enables the life I want. The status opens doors to do the work I want.

What I actually value:

Research potential on a daily basis. Am I learning something new? Am I exploring ideas that haven't been tried? Am I pushing boundaries, even incrementally?

Strategic work over tactical work. Am I making decisions that matter, or executing decisions others made? Am I defining direction, or following it?

Inspiring others and setting conceptual guidelines. When I built the declarative agent framework, what felt meaningful wasn't the technical achievement. It was creating a novel way to think about agent orchestration. Setting a conceptual guideline for how we can improve software development.

That's what I care about. Creating new ways of thinking about problems. Contributing ideas that others can build on.

13.5   The 4AM Question

What drives me when I can't sleep at 4am, thinking about a problem?

Not career advancement. Not performance reviews. Not even the satisfaction of solving the problem.

What drives me is the desire to find optimal solutions. To understand our universe. To simplify complex systems into elegant abstractions.

It's the same thing that drove me at 10 years old when I said I wanted to be an inventor. Thinking of Doc Brown inventing the flux capacitor or Albert Einstein developing the theory of relativity. Not because I wanted to invent time travel specifically, but because I wanted to create novel devices and novel theories.

That hasn't changed in 38 years. The specific problems changed. The fundamental drive didn't.

13.5.1 What Would I Do If Money Wasn't a Factor?

I would work only on contributing to human knowledge from a theoretical point of view. Pure research. Computer science and mathematics.

Not building products. Not creating commercial value. Just understanding for understanding's sake. Publishing science that other scientists use to continue research. Making even just one step forward toward something meaningful for the human species.

That's my true purpose. Money and status are just part of the societal establishment we created. They enable the work, but they're not why I do the work.

13.6 The Star Trek Lens: AI as Alien Species

My thinking about technology was shaped by *Star Trek: The Next Generation*. Not just entertainment—philosophy about humanity's relationship with technology.

Here's how I see AI: it's a bit like an alien species that's coexisting with us. We're exploring it the same way the Enterprise explored strange new worlds.

During all these years, my work in one way or another has contributed to adding another level of abstraction to automation. Each framework I built, each system I designed, moved us one step further from direct manipulation of bits toward expressing intent at higher levels.

The declarative agent framework I built continues this pattern. You don't tell the computer how to execute agent workflows. You describe what the agent should accomplish, and the system figures out execution.

This is exploration. Understanding what's possible when you give intelligence—even artificial intelligence—the right structure to operate within. Discovering what emerges when you combine human intent with machine capability.

Star Trek was optimistic about technology augmenting humanity, not replacing it. The Enterprise had a computer that could answer any factual question instantly. But humans still made the decisions. Still explored. Still wondered. Still created meaning.

That's the future I'm building toward. Not humans competing with AI, but humans and AI as collaborative species exploring what becomes possible together.

13.7   What Makes Work Meaningful

Let me tell you about a moment in my work that crystallized this for me.

I was presenting the declarative agent framework to a group of engineers from different teams. Not executives—working engineers who would actually use the system.

One engineer said: "This changes how I think about building agents. I can express workflows I couldn't express before."

That moment. That's why I do this.

Not because I'd built something technically impressive—though it was. Not because it would be adopted organization-wide—though it has been. But because I'd created a conceptual tool that changed how someone thought about their work.

I realized what I was doing was beyond any coding or architecting. I was inspiring others. I was setting conceptual guidelines for how we improve software development.

That's meaning. That's purpose. That's what makes work worth doing regardless of salary or status.

13.7.1 Why Patents Matter to Me

People ask why I file patents. The provisional patents I have don't generate revenue. They're defensive, not offensive.

But they matter to me as recognition of contributions. It's not easy at large organizations to get your ideas patented. The process requires proving the work is genuinely novel, that it advances the field, that it's worth protecting.

Getting patents approved says: your innovations matter. Not just to the company, but to the broader field. Someone evaluated your work and said "yes, this is a contribution."

That recognition matters when your purpose is contributing to human knowledge.

13.7.2 Why This Book

I'm writing this book for several reasons, and career positioning is only one of them.

The deeper reasons:

I see colleagues struggling to adapt. More than ever now. People with strong backgrounds—currently at Meta, Apple, Google, Amazon—failing job interviews because we're looking for different skills than we looked for five years ago.

I see people lost since COVID ended. The remote work shift disrupted careers. People who thrived in office environments struggling with remote work, or vice versa. People who got fired and can't find jobs doing what they love.

I see very strong candidates struggling. Not because they're not capable, but because they don't recognize the pattern. They think AI is different from previous automation waves. They're paralyzed by fear rather than energized by opportunity.

I've been always ready for this because I've seen it over and over. I feel I can help by sharing the pattern, showing that adaptation is learnable, proving that it's never too late.

But there's another reason, more personal:

This book is self-reflection. Understanding what I've been doing and where I'm going. It serves me as a starting point, a clean slate.

After 26 years of detour through industry, I'm finally positioned to do the research work I wanted to do at 22. This book is me understanding that journey, making sense of the pattern, articulating what I've learned.

Writing is how I think. This book is thinking in public about what matters, what I've learned, where I'm going.

13.8   The Bigger Question We're Avoiding

All the advice about skills and positioning assumes work is fundamentally about economic productivity. About being valuable to employers. About career success.

But what if that's not the point?

13.8.1   What Humans Reserve for Themselves

Bill Gates said something interesting that people often misunderstand: "People don't want to watch robots play baseball."

Think about what this reveals. We could build robots that play baseball perfectly. Better than any human. Faster, stronger, more accurate, never injured, never tired.

We don't want to watch them.

Why? Because baseball isn't about optimal performance. It's about human struggle, human achievement, human drama. The imperfection is the point. The possibility of failure makes success meaningful.

Same with music. We can synthesize perfect music—every note mathematically optimal, every frequency precisely tuned. We prefer human musicians. Why? Because the humanity matters more than the perfection.

Same with art. AI can generate technically impressive images. Human-made art sells for millions. Not because it's technically superior. Because it carries human intent, human meaning, human expression.

We value human creation not despite its imperfections, but because of them. Because imperfection signals genuine human effort, human choice, human meaning.

13.8.2   What This Means for Work

If we value human baseball over robot baseball, human music over synthesized perfection, human art over AI generation—what does that tell us about work?

Maybe the question isn't "what work can humans still do?" but "what work do humans WANT to do?"

Maybe productivity isn't the point. Maybe meaning is.

13.9   My Personal Reckoning With This

For 26 years, I optimized for productivity. Building systems that served millions of users. Writing code that processed billions of transactions. Creating frameworks that multiplied team effectiveness.

All valuable. All productive. All economically justified.

But not what I actually wanted to be doing.

13.9.1   What I Wanted at 10

When I was 10 years old, if you asked me what I wanted to be when I grew up, I would say: "I want to be an inventor."

Not "I want to be a software engineer." Not "I want to build software." I want to be an inventor.

Thinking of Doc Brown inventing the flux capacitor in *Back to the Future*. Albert Einstein developing the theory of relativity. Not because I wanted to invent time travel specifically, but because I wanted to create novel devices and novel theories.

I wanted to understand how the universe works. To discover things nobody knew before. To contribute to humanity's knowledge in fundamental ways.

That's what a 10-year-old me understood about purpose.

13.9.2 The 26-Year Detour

At 22, reading *"Investigar en España es llorar"* ("To do research in Spain is to cry"), I understood the economic and systemic barriers ahead. Research in Spain meant decades of struggle. Limited funding. Few opportunities. No clear path.

I chose the viable path instead of the desired path. Came to the United States at 22. Built a career in software engineering. Not my first choice, but the practical one.

For nearly two decades, I channeled intellectual curiosity into production systems. Novel algorithms for real problems. Technical challenges with constraints. Always knowing that formal research remained out of reach without credentials.

But the desire never disappeared.

13.9.3 What Those Years Actually Gave Me

Industry experience taught me something pure researchers often lack: how to build things that actually work. How to translate theory into practice. How to solve problems with real constraints—budget, time, organizational dynamics, technical limitations.

Pure researchers can be brilliant theoretically but struggle with practical implementation. I can do both because I spent 26 years learning to build real systems.

That perspective is valuable. It informs my research now in ways that wouldn't be possible without the detour.

But it was still a detour. Not the path I'd have chosen if I'd had the means and opportunity at 22.

13.10 What I Value Now: The Research Potential

What I value most is the research potential on a daily basis.

Am I learning something new? Am I exploring ideas that haven't been tried? Am I pushing boundaries, even incrementally?

When I built the declarative agent framework, the meaningful part wasn't the technical achievement. It was creating a novel way to define agents and pipelines. Something that didn't exist before. A contribution to how we think about orchestrating AI systems.

When I wrote the academic paper, the meaningful part wasn't publishing—it was articulating ideas clearly enough that others could build on them. Contributing to the conversation in the field.

When I file patents, what matters is the recognition that my contributions are genuinely novel. Not just commercially valuable, but advancing what's possible.

13.10.1 Strategic Work Over Tactical Work

The other thing I value: am I doing strategic work or tactical work?

Strategic work: defining what to build and why. Making architectural decisions. Creating frameworks that enable others. Setting direction.

Tactical work: implementing features someone else specified. Following patterns someone else established. Executing plans someone else made.

I can do tactical work. I did it for years. I'm good at it. But it doesn't fulfill me the way strategic work does.

That's not about ego. It's about how I'm wired. I'm driven by understanding, by creating new approaches, by contributing to how we think about problems.

Tactical work is necessary. Someone has to do it. But it's not what gets me out of bed at 4am thinking about solutions.

13.11 The Meaning Pattern Across History

Let me show you something about how human work has evolved.

13.11.1 The Historical Progression

Agricultural age: 90% of humans farmed for survival. Work was about not starving. Meaning came from community, family, religion—things outside work.

Industrial age: 40% in manufacturing. Work was about production and wages. Meaning still came mostly from outside work—though craftsmanship mattered to some.

Information age: 60% in knowledge work. Work became where many people found meaning—solving problems, building systems, creating value. But still constrained by economic necessity.

AI age: ???

Here's the question: if AI handles most productive work, where do humans find meaning?

Maybe the answer is: *in work we choose because we want to do it, not because we need to do it for survival.*

13.11.2 What Drives Me Now

I work on AI not for the salary—though I'm well compensated. Not for status—though I have recognition.

I work on AI because:

- It's intellectually challenging in ways that satisfy my need to understand complex systems

- It contributes to how we think about intelligence, both artificial and human

- It positions me to do the research I wanted to do at 22

- It lets me inspire others and contribute to their growth

- It's exploring strange new worlds—understanding an alien intelligence we're creating

None of those are about productivity or economic value. They're about meaning.

13.12 When You're 70: The Legacy Question

When I'm 70, what do I want to have contributed?

Definitely papers. Books. Students I mentored.

Not the systems I built—those will be obsolete. Not the code I wrote—that will be replaced. Not the money I earned—that will be spent.

But the ideas I contributed? Those persist. The students I helped? They continue contributing. The frameworks for thinking I created? Others build on them.

That's legacy. Not what you accumulated, but what you contributed.

13.12.1 Why This Matters for AI Discussion

We're having the wrong conversation about AI and employment.

The conversation is: "Will AI eliminate jobs? How do we prepare for mass unemployment?"

The better conversation: "If AI handles productive work, what will humans do with their time? What's worth doing beyond economic necessity?"

This isn't utopian speculation. It's practical question. As AI handles more tasks, we're forced to confront: what makes work meaningful beyond the paycheck?

Some people find meaning in their work. Others work to fund their actual interests outside work. Both are valid.

But AI is revealing that productivity—economic output—isn't the ultimate measure of human value. It's one measure. Maybe not even the most important one.

13.13 The Reframe

Throughout this book, I've given you tactical advice. How to develop judgment. How to cultivate creativity. How to build relationships. How to learn continuously. How to position yourself strategically.

All of that matters. Those skills will make you valuable in an AI-augmented economy.

But there's a deeper question underneath all the tactics:

What do you actually want to do with your life?

Not "what job will survive AI?" but "what work would you do if AI handled all the necessary-but-not-meaningful tasks?"

For me, it's research. Contributing to computational science and mathematics. Understanding intelligence—artificial and human. Teaching others. Writing.

For you, it might be completely different. Building things. Helping people. Creating art. Solving specific domain problems. Leading teams. Mentoring.

13.13.1   AI as Liberation, Not Threat

Here's the reframe: AI isn't taking away work. It's taking away the work we only did because it was necessary.

What remains is the work we'd choose to do anyway. Work that's meaningful beyond economic value.

If you love writing code for its own sake—the elegance of a well-designed algorithm, the satisfaction of solving puzzles—AI doesn't threaten that. You can still code. But now you can focus on the interesting problems rather than the routine ones.

If you love helping people—solving their problems, making their lives easier—AI doesn't threaten that. It gives you tools to help more people more effectively.

If you love understanding how systems work—the intellectual challenge of complex domains—AI doesn't threaten that. It lets you explore more complex domains faster.

AI threatens the work you only did for money. The work that was economically necessary but not personally meaningful.

And maybe that's not a threat. Maybe that's liberation.

13.14   What I'm Building Toward

At 48, I'm finally positioned to do the work I wanted to do at 22.

I'm writing academic papers on agent orchestration systems. Contributing to how the field thinks about deploying AI at scale. Filing patents on novel approaches to AI infrastructure.

I'm mentoring engineers on how to work with AI effectively. Teaching them not just technical skills but judgment, strategy, how to navigate careers.

I'm building production systems that demonstrate how AI should augment humans rather than replace them. Creating frameworks that multiply human effectiveness rather than eliminating human involvement.

And I'm writing this book. Sharing what I've learned. Contributing to the conversation about how we navigate technological change.

None of this is about maximizing income or status. It's about doing work that feels meaningful. Work that contributes. Work that aligns with my purpose.

13.14.1 What Automation Actually Enables

If AI automates the work I only did for money, I get to focus on the work I actually care about.

That's not unemployment. That's the opportunity to align work with purpose.

For 26 years, I did software engineering because it paid well and I was good at it. Now I'm doing research because it's what I actually want to contribute.

AI didn't eliminate my options. It expanded them. By making execution less valuable, it made strategic and creative work more valuable. And strategic and creative work is what I actually wanted to be doing anyway.

13.15 The Question for You

So here's what I'm asking you to consider:

What would you do with your time if AI handled all the execution work? Not just career positioning—though that matters. But fundamentally: what work would you choose if economic necessity wasn't the primary driver?

Because that's where we're heading. Not immediately, but directionally. As AI handles more tasks, economic productivity becomes less about human execution and more about human judgment, creativity, and meaning-making.

13.15.1   Maybe the Anxiety Is Misplaced

The anxiety about AI eliminating jobs assumes work is primarily about economic survival. That losing your job means losing purpose.

But what if work is about meaning, not just money? What if the jobs AI eliminates are the ones that were never meaningful anyway—just economically necessary?

What if AI forces us to confront what we actually value about work, what we'd choose to do if we had the choice?

That's not threatening. That's clarifying.

13.15.2   The Skills Still Matter

Let me be clear: I'm not saying skills don't matter. Everything in Chapters 7-12—judgment, creativity, relationships, learning—those remain essential.

But the ultimate question isn't "what skills keep me employed?" It's "what do I want to contribute?"

The skills enable the contribution. They're means, not ends.

Understanding that distinction changes how you approach career decisions. You're not optimizing for job security. You're optimizing for meaningful work that aligns with purpose.

And paradoxically, that makes you more valuable economically. Because people who work with purpose, who care about outcomes beyond metrics, who contribute meaning—they create value that's hard to replicate.

13.16   The Pattern Continues

Human computers did calculations for money. When computers automated calculation, some became programmers. Not because programming paid better—though it did. But because programming was more intellectually interesting.

The work evolved from executing calculations to designing what to calculate. From following procedures to creating procedures. From doing necessary work to doing meaningful work.

The same pattern is happening now. AI automates execution. Humans move to judgment, creativity, strategy. Not just because those skills are economically valuable—though they are. But because they're more meaningful.

Work keeps evolving toward what humans actually want to do when given the choice.

That's the optimistic interpretation of AI's impact. Not that humans become obsolete, but that humans finally get to focus on work that's meaningful rather than just necessary.

The next chapter explores what future we're actually building. Two paths forward. Which one we get depends on choices being made right now—by companies, by individuals, by society.

And you're part of those choices. Whether you realize it or not, how you respond to AI shapes which future we get.

That's what we explore next.

Chapter 14

The Future We Choose

14.1 Two Paths Diverge

We're at a decision point. Not a distant, theoretical one—a decision being made right now, in boardrooms and home offices, in the code we write and the skills we build. The choices of 2025 and 2026 will determine which of two very different futures becomes reality.

Both futures have advanced AI. Both have automation handling most execution work. Both have transformed how we live and work.

But they diverge sharply in what they value, how they treat human contribution, and what kind of life becomes possible.

Let me show you what each looks like—not as abstraction, but as lived experience.

14.2 Future A: The Drift

14.2.1 A Day in 2035: Michael

The notification wakes Michael at 6:47am: *"Application Status Update: Position Filled."* That's the fourteenth rejection this week. He doesn't bother checking which company—they blur together now.

He's forty years old. Eighteen years of software engineering experience. Stanford CS degree, class of 2017. A résumé that would have commanded $400,000 total compensation in 2025.

But it's 2035, and AI screening systems process his application in 0.3

seconds before any human sees it. The algorithms scan for keywords he doesn't have: *neural architecture oversight, synthetic reasoning auditor, human-AI workflow designer.* His résumé says *senior software engineer* and lists languages, frameworks, systems he built. The algorithms see: *legacy skills, retraining risk, cultural mismatch.*

Six months ago, he was still employed. Senior Engineer at a mid-sized fintech company, twelve years tenure. Good performance reviews. Respected by his team.

Then the restructuring memo arrived.

"To remain competitive, we're transitioning to AI-first development. This enables us to maintain output quality while right-sizing our engineering organization."

Right-sizing meant sixty percent headcount reduction. The company kept engineers who'd been using AI tools extensively for two years—who'd rebuilt their workflows around AI assistance, who thought in terms of AI orchestration rather than direct implementation. Michael had used Copilot occasionally, found it helpful for boilerplate, but never fundamentally changed how he worked.

He'd been skeptical. Cautious. Waiting to see if the AI hype was real before committing to a new way of working.

By the time he realized it was real, thousands of engineers with similar résumés were flooding the job market. All competing for a shrinking pool of positions that still wanted traditional engineering skills.

Now he takes contract work through a gig platform. API integrations. Database migrations. Legacy system maintenance—the work AI handles poorly because the systems are old, undocumented, and weird. It pays forty percent of his previous salary. No benefits. No stability. Each contract might be his last as AI gets better at handling edge cases.

His daughter asks why he seems sad. He doesn't know how to explain that he's watching his professional identity dissolve, skill by skill, year by year.

The worst part isn't the money. It's the uselessness. He spent two decades building expertise that turned out to be a commodity. He executes tasks that feel mechanical, meaningless, interchangeable. He's not building anything. He's maintaining someone else's legacy while waiting for AI to learn how to replace him entirely.

14.2.2   What Michael's World Looks Like

Michael isn't alone. His world is full of people like him—competent professionals who optimized for the wrong metrics, who built expertise in execution rather than judgment, who waited too long to adapt.

From the outside, 2035 looks prosperous. The economy is productive. AI systems optimize everything from supply chains to medical diagnoses. Technology is everywhere, seamlessly integrated, impressively capable.

But there's a fracture running through society.

On one side: those who learned to work *with* AI early. Who repositioned themselves as orchestrators, evaluators, decision-makers. Who provide the judgment, creativity, and human connection that AI still can't replicate. They're thriving—earning more than ever, doing more interesting work, freed from tedium to focus on problems that matter.

On the other side: those who competed with AI on execution, or resisted it entirely, or simply moved too slowly. They're scrambling for diminishing opportunities, watching their skills depreciate faster than they can acquire new ones, trapped in a downward spiral where lack of resources prevents the retraining that might reverse their decline.

The gap compounds. Those doing well can invest in continuous learning, take sabbaticals to acquire new capabilities, afford the coaching and credentials that signal adaptability. Those struggling work multiple gigs with no time for education, no savings for career investment, no network to surface opportunities.

Healthcare is AI-optimized: accurate, efficient, available. But rushed. When Michael's mother needed help understanding her diagnosis—not the facts, but what they *meant* for how she should live—the AI provided information. It couldn't provide comfort. The human doctors were overloaded, incentivized for throughput, trained to defer to AI recommendations.

Work has become transactional everywhere. AI systems assign tasks, evaluate output, determine compensation. They're fair in ways human managers weren't—no favoritism, no bias, no politics. But they can't inspire. Can't mentor. Can't recognize when someone needs encouragement rather than a performance improvement plan.

The worst part isn't unemployment. It's *meaninglessness*. Humans haven't been eliminated—they've been diminished. Reduced to implementing AI decisions, executing AI plans, serving AI systems. Comfortable enough. Needs met. But not *creating*. Not contributing. Not essential.

That's the dystopia. Not extinction—irrelevance.

14.3 Future B: The Renaissance

14.3.1 A Day in 2035: Sarah

Sarah's morning starts with coffee and a decision.

Overnight, her AI collaborators generated five architectural proposals for a distributed system. Each approach is technically sound—the AI has analyzed latency requirements, security constraints, regulatory compliance, cost projections, team capabilities. The documentation is thorough. The tradeoffs are clearly laid out.

The AI can tell her which option optimizes for each variable. It can't tell her which variables *matter most* for this company, this team, this moment in the market.

That's her job.

She's forty years old. Eighteen years of engineering experience—but unlike Michael in the other timeline, she rebuilt her career twice. First in 2025, when she forced herself to master AI-assisted development even though it felt awkward and slow at first. Then in 2029, when she shifted from AI-assisted *coding* to AI-assisted architecture—from directing AI implementations to evaluating AI proposals and making strategic technical decisions.

She spends two hours with the proposals. Not checking the technical work—the AI is reliable for that. Reading between the lines. Which approach will the infrastructure team actually embrace? Which aligns with where the CEO wants to take the company? Which creates optionality for pivots they might need in eighteen months?

Her recommendation goes out at 9am. The AI team begins implementation. She'll review their work later, but her primary value has already been delivered: judgment about what to build and why.

By 10am, she's in collaboration mode—a working session with engineers in Singapore, designers in Stockholm, product managers in São Paulo. The AI handles real-time translation, transcription, action item tracking. Sarah focuses on something AI still can't do well: navigating disagreement. The Singapore team has concerns about the timeline. The Stockholm designers want more iteration time. The product managers are under pressure from sales.

Sarah doesn't resolve this by finding the "optimal" answer—there isn't one. She resolves it by understanding each perspective deeply enough to find the path that everyone can commit to. By reading frustration in someone's voice and addressing it before it becomes opposition. By knowing when to push and when to yield.

Afternoons are for mentorship. Junior engineers don't need her to teach syntax—AI tutors do that better than any human. They need her to teach *judgment*. How to evaluate AI suggestions. How to recognize when "technically correct" is strategically wrong. How to develop the instincts that only come from experience.

Her mentee today is struggling with a decision the AI can't make: whether to leave his current role for a startup opportunity. The AI can list pros and cons, calculate expected value, assess risk tolerance. It can't understand what he *actually wants* from his career, what he'll regret, what aligns with who he's trying to become.

Sarah can. Not because she's smarter than the AI, but because she's human. Because she's made similar decisions and lived with the consequences. Because she can hear what he's not saying and reflect it back to him.

Her work is meaningful. She's contributing—not just to her company, but to the people she develops, the decisions she improves, the judgment she cultivates in others. She has time for education, creativity, family. The parts of her job that were tedious—the documentation, the boilerplate, the routine decisions—AI handles those. What's left is the work she'd choose to do anyway.

14.3.2 What Sarah's World Looks Like

Sarah's world made different choices.

Companies recognized early that AI's value wasn't replacing humans—it was *freeing* humans to do what they do best. The firms that thrived weren't those that cut headcount fastest. They were those that redeployed human talent to judgment, creativity, and relationship-intensive work while AI handled execution.

The economic logic became clear by 2028: companies that "replaced" humans got short-term efficiency gains but lost the capacity to innovate, to navigate ambiguity, to build cultures that attract talent. Companies that "augmented" humans developed sustainable advantages—institutional wisdom, adaptive capability, human networks that created value AI couldn't replicate.

Society reorganized around this insight. Education shifted from knowledge transfer—AI handles that—to capability development. Teaching people to learn continuously, evaluate information critically, collaborate effectively, make decisions under uncertainty.

Healthcare combines AI precision with human presence. The AI diagnoses accurately and recommends treatment optimally. Human practitioners provide what AI can't: the conversation that helps patients understand what their diagnosis *means*, the emotional support that affects healing, the judgment calls that require understanding a patient's values and circumstances.

Work is meaningful across most of the economy. Not because every job is fascinating, but because the meaningless parts have been automated away. What remains is work that requires human capabilities—and humans find satisfaction in exercising capabilities that matter.

The transition wasn't smooth. The 2020s and early 2030s were turbulent—rapid job transformation, political conflict over AI governance, anxiety and displacement. But society chose to invest in adaptation rather than resistance. In human development rather than human replacement.

It chose the future where humans remain essential—not despite AI, but because of what AI revealed: that human value was never in execution. It was in judgment, creativity, connection, meaning-making. AI made that clear by taking over everything else.

14.4 The Hinge Point

Both futures start from the same technology. The same AI capabilities. The same potential for transformation.

The difference is choices—made by individuals, organizations, and societies between 2025 and 2030.

We're in that window now.

14.4.1 Individual Choices

Every day, you're choosing which future you inhabit.

The resistance path: Refuse to engage with AI tools. Insist on doing things the way you've always done them. Compete on execution speed and traditional skills. This path leads reliably to Michael's outcome—not because you're incapable, but because you're optimizing for metrics that are rapidly devaluing.

The competition path: Adopt AI tools but focus on producing more output faster. Try to out-execute the competition. This is better than resistance, but still the wrong game. You're racing against exponential improvement. Even if you win today, you'll lose eventually—and you'll burn out in the process, never building the capabilities that would keep you valuable long-term.

The partnership path: Use AI to handle execution while you focus on judgment, creativity, strategy, relationships. Develop the capabilities AI can't replicate. Position yourself as the human who makes AI useful, not the human AI makes unnecessary.

Michael took the resistance path, then switched to competition too late. Sarah took the partnership path early and kept evolving.

The choice is available to you right now. Today. Not after you finish the current project or when you have more time or once you understand AI better. Now.

14.4.2 Organizational Choices

Companies are choosing which future they create.

The replacement strategy: See AI as cost reduction. Calculate how many humans can be eliminated. Optimize for productivity metrics. Treat workers as expensive resources to minimize.

This works short-term. Margins improve. Shareholders approve. But by 2030, these companies face innovation deficits (no human judgment to break patterns), institutional amnesia (no accumulated wisdom about what works and why), culture collapse (talented people avoid companies that treat humans as disposable), and brittleness (systems optimized for efficiency can't adapt when conditions change).

The augmentation strategy: See AI as amplification. Invest in tools *and* in training people to use them well. Redeploy humans to judgment, strategy, creativity, relationships. Understand that efficiency gains mean nothing without the human wisdom to direct them toward valuable outcomes.

These companies sacrifice some short-term efficiency for long-term capability. By 2030, they're the ones still innovating, still attracting talent, still able to navigate uncertainty. They're the ones building the future where work remains meaningful.

14.4.3   Societal Choices

Societies are choosing which future becomes widespread.

Some societies optimize for productivity metrics—GDP growth, automation rates, efficiency indices. They let market forces determine how AI reshapes work, assuming optimal outcomes will emerge from competition.

Other societies optimize for human flourishing—meaningful work, capability development, social cohesion. They invest in education that develops judgment rather than transfers knowledge. They create incentives for augmentation over replacement. They ensure the benefits of AI-driven productivity are broadly shared rather than concentrated.

The first approach may produce more aggregate wealth. The second produces more aggregate wellbeing. They're not the same thing.

You influence societal choices too—through how you vote, what you advocate for, which companies you support with your labor and your purchases. These feel like small actions. They compound into the future we get.

14.5   Making the Choice

This chapter isn't just analysis. It's a decision point.

You've read the scenarios. You've seen where different paths lead. You understand—at least intellectually—what determines which future becomes real.

Now: what will you actually do?

Not abstractly. Not eventually. What will you do *tomorrow* that moves you toward Sarah's future rather than Michael's?

Start using AI tools seriously if you haven't. Not as novelty, but as core workflow.

Identify one capability that's uniquely human—judgment, creativity, relationship-building—and invest in developing it.

Look at your current work and ask: am I building skills that compound with AI advancement, or skills that compete against it?

Find one person who's struggling with the transition and help them. Mentorship builds the future where humans support each other through change.

The choices feel small. They're not. They're the mechanism by which one future becomes real and the other remains hypothetical.

Michael made small choices—to wait, to be skeptical, to keep doing what had always worked. The choices accumulated into a life he didn't want.

Sarah made small choices too—to learn early, to rebuild continuously, to focus on what AI couldn't replace. Those choices accumulated into a life of meaning and contribution.

Your choices start accumulating tomorrow.

Which future are you building?

Chapter 15

Conclusion: The Human Advantage

15.1 The Pattern Proven

We began this book with a question: what happens when technology threatens to make humans obsolete?

The human computers of the 1940s faced that question directly. Electronic computers really did replace their work completely. The predictions of obsolescence were technically accurate.

And yet the Adaptation Pattern proved more powerful than the predictions of doom.

The Power Principle: ENIAC exceeded all expectations. The technology was more powerful than anyone imagined.

The Transformation Principle: The work didn't disappear. It multiplied and evolved. From thousands of human computers to millions of programmers and engineers.

The Early Mover Principle: Grace Hopper, Margaret Hamilton, Dorothy Vaughan—the pioneers who adapted early built careers spanning decades.

The Messy Middle Principle: The transition was neither smooth nor fair. But the overall direction was clear.

The Human Core Principle: The value that remained was judgment, creativity, and understanding. Not calculation speed, but knowing what to calculate. Not competing with machines, but directing them toward human purposes.

I've lived through this pattern four times in my own career. Each wave followed the same arc: fear, then transition, then expansion. Those who recognized the pattern adapted. Those who adapted thrived.

Now it's your turn.

15.2   Your Playbook

The Adaptation Pattern is your playbook for navigating the transition happening right now.

Start learning and using AI tools immediately. Don't wait for perfect understanding. Early adoption gives you pattern recognition before the rush.

Discover your purpose—what work would you do if AI handled all the necessary-but-not-meaningful tasks? That's the work to position yourself for.

Reject catastrophism. Yes, work is transforming. No, humans aren't becoming obsolete. Clear thinking about the actual pattern helps everyone.

Invest deliberately in judgment, creativity, relationships, and learning agility. These are the skills that never depreciate. These are what make you irreplaceable.

And recognize the urgency. The companies building AI spent years in development before public release. By the time you see capabilities, they're already years ahead internally. Your window for adaptation is shorter than it was for previous waves.

The question isn't whether to adapt. It's whether you'll lead or follow.

15.3   The Deeper Message

Being human was never about tasks. We've conflated "doing work" with "being valuable" for so long that we forgot what actually makes us human.

The fear of AI isn't really about losing jobs. It's about losing our sense of purpose because we've tied our identity to our productivity.

But as we explored in Chapter 1, the value of human computers wasn't their calculation speed—it was their judgment, understanding, and accountability when stakes were highest.

Being human is about judgment in ambiguous situations where competing values must be balanced. Empathy that goes beyond data. Caring about outcomes in ways that matter beyond optimization metrics. Love, connection, and meaning in our work and relationships.

The questions that matter are never "how fast can you do this?" but "should you do this at all?" and "what does this mean for the people affected?"

By automating tasks, AI strips away the illusion that our value comes from repetitive execution. It forces us to confront what we actually bring that machines cannot: meaning-making, ethical reasoning, contextual understanding.

When machines handle execution, humans are freed to handle intention. And that's where our real value has always been.

15.4   The Human Advantage

We're not better calculators than machines. We never were.

We're the only ones who care why the calculations matter. Who understand context beyond data. Who exercise judgment about what's worth calculating in the first place. Who take responsibility when calculations are wrong.

That's enough. That's everything.

That's what remains when machines do everything else: the fact that we care why it matters. The judgment to know when "technically correct" isn't actually right. The humanity to understand that some decisions require empathy, not just optimization.

Humans are adaptable by nature. It's our evolutionary advantage. We've never been made obsolete by our tools because we're the ones who decide what the tools should do and what outcomes matter.

Tasks change. The need for judgment, context, meaning, and accountability doesn't.

15.5 Our Next Chapters

At 48, after 26 years of detour through industry, I'm finally positioned to do what I wanted to do at 22: research and teaching. Contributing to computer science. Publishing papers. Teaching engineers how to work with AI while maintaining human judgment. Building frameworks that keep humans essential rather than optional.

This book is part of that mission. Not just sharing what I've learned, but contributing to the conversation about how we navigate technological change without losing what makes us human.

Your story is just beginning.

You've seen the pattern. You understand the skills. You have the playbook.

Now you get to choose: which future will you build through your daily decisions?

Will you resist AI and struggle? Will you compete with AI and burn out? Or will you partner with AI and thrive?

The skills are learnable—I proved that getting degrees at 46-48 while working full-time. The future is navigable—I proved that adapting through multiple waves while building the career I wanted.

If I can do it, you can do it.

15.6 The Invitation

We built machines to do our work. Now we're free to do our purpose.

Not by competing with AI on AI's terms. But by embracing what makes you irreplaceable: your judgment, your creativity, your relationships, your ability to learn and adapt.

The transition is happening now. The choices are being made now. The future is being built now.

I'm building a future where AI amplifies human capability while humans provide the judgment and meaning that make AI useful rather than just powerful. Where we use machines to free ourselves for work that matters, not to make ourselves obsolete.

That's Future B. The renaissance.

You can build that future too. Through your choices. Through your adaptations. Through recognizing the pattern and acting on it.

The strategy works. The skills are learnable. The future is navigable.

The question isn't whether you'll survive this transition.

The question is: what will you build with it?

Welcome to the next chapter. Yours is just beginning.

Engage!

References

1X Technologies. *NEO Humanoid Robot*. Teleoperated humanoid robot for household assistance. 2025.

Aaker, Jennifer. "Human First: Designing Artificial Intelligence That Elevates Us". In: *Stanford Graduate School of Business Insights* (2024). Discussion of human-centered AI design emphasizing authenticity, boldness, and human values. URL: https://www.gsb.stanford.edu/insights/human-first-designing-artificial-intelligence-elevates-us.

Amazon Web Services. *Amazon S3 Launch*. Launch of Amazon Simple Storage Service, pioneering cloud storage. 2006.

Chase, Harrison. *LangChain: Building Applications with LLMs Through Composability*. Python framework for building LLM applications. 2023. URL: https://github.com/langchain-ai/langchain.

Daunis, Ivan. *A Declarative Language for Building and Orchestrating LLM-Powered Agent Workflows*. 2025. arXiv: 2512.19769 [cs.AI]. URL: https://arxiv.org/abs/2512.19769.

Daunis Llobet, Ivan et al. *System and Method for Personalized Women's Health Management Using Smart Earrings AI and Mobile Application*. U.S. Provisional Patent No. 63/709,694. Filed October 21, 2024. Oct. 2024.

— *Wearable Devices Using Machine Learned Models for Individual-Specific Biometric Tracking and Outcome Predictions*. U.S. Provisional Patent No. 63/709,579. Filed October 21, 2024. Oct. 2024.

Deng, Jia et al. "ImageNet: A Large-Scale Hierarchical Image Database". In: *IEEE Conference on Computer Vision and Pattern Recognition*

(2009). ImageNet dataset that enabled modern computer vision, pp. 248–255.

Doidge, Norman. "The Brain That Changes Itself: Stories of Personal Triumph from the Frontiers of Brain Science". In: *Penguin Books* (2007). Research on neuroplasticity and lifelong learning capacity.

Ericsson, K. Anders, Ralf Th. Krampe, and Clemens Tesch-Römer. "The Role of Deliberate Practice in the Acquisition of Expert Performance". In: *Psychological Review* 100.3 (1993). Research on how expertise develops through practice, pp. 363–406.

Gates, Bill. *Bill Gates on AI: Humans Won't Be Needed 'For Most Things'*. Interview on The Tonight Show with Jimmy Fallon, NBC. Statement on artificial intelligence and future of work. Feb. 2025.

Goldman Sachs Research. *The Economic Impact of Artificial Intelligence.* Aggregate labor market impacts from AI remain negligible. Goldman Sachs, 2024.

Goldstine, Herman H. and Adele Goldstine. "The ENIAC: First General-Purpose Electronic Computer". In: *Mathematical Tables and Other Aids to Computation* 2.15 (1946). Technical description of ENIAC and its capabilities, pp. 97–110.

Grier, David Alan. *When Computers Were Human.* Comprehensive history of human computers from 1600s to 1960s. Princeton University Press, 2005.

Hamilton, Margaret H. "Apollo Flight Software Development". In: *IEEE Software* (1971). Software engineering for Apollo missions.

Hopper, Grace. *The Education of a Computer.* Early work on compiler development. ACM, 1952.

Humane Inc. *Humane AI Pin Product Launch and Market Reception.* Wearable AI device attempting to replace smartphones. 2024.

Kinreich, Sivan et al. "Brain-to-Brain Synchrony during Naturalistic Social Interactions". In: *Scientific Reports* 7 (2017). Gamma-wave neural synchrony observed in couples but not strangers during social interactions, p. 17060. DOI: 10.1038/s41598-017-17339-5.

Krizhevsky, Alex, Ilya Sutskever, and Geoffrey E. Hinton. "ImageNet Classification with Deep Convolutional Neural Networks". In: *Advances in Neural Information Processing Systems*. Breakthrough paper that launched deep learning revolution. 2012, pp. 1097–1105.

Light, Jennifer S. "When Computers Were Women". In: *Technology and Culture* 40.3 (1999). Historical analysis of human computers and early electronic computing, pp. 455–483.

MIT Sloan Management Review. "AI Investment Returns: Industry Survey". In: (2024). 95% of organizations reporting zero return on AI investments.

Reinero, Diego A., Suzanne Dikker, and Jay J. Van Bavel. "Inter-brain Synchrony in Teams Predicts Collective Performance". In: *Social Cognitive and Affective Neuroscience* 16.1-2 (Jan. 2021). Study of 174 participants showing inter-brain synchrony predicts team performance in problem-solving tasks, pp. 43–57. DOI: 10.1093/scan/nsaa135.

Shetterly, Margot Lee. *Hidden Figures: The American Dream and the Untold Story of the Black Women Mathematicians Who Helped Win the Space Race*. Story of Katherine Johnson, Dorothy Vaughan, and Mary Jackson at NASA. William Morrow, 2016.

Tolle, Eckhart. *The Power of Now: A Guide to Spiritual Enlightenment*. Quote about instability and peace. New World Library, 2004.

U.S. Bureau of Labor Statistics. *Computing Occupations Historical Data*. 450,000 workers in information technology, first official Census data on computing occupations. 1970.

U.S. Census Bureau. *Computer and Information Technology Occupations*. 4.6 million Americans employed in IT occupations. 2014.

WorkOS. *AI Initiative Abandonment Rates in Enterprise*. 42% of companies abandoned most AI initiatives in 2025, up from 17% in 2024. 2025.

Index

About the Author

Ivan Daunis is a computer scientist and AI engineer with over 30 years of experience in software development. He currently leads agentic AI initiatives at PayPal, focusing on declarative approaches to AI agent orchestration.

Ivan's career spans multiple waves of technological evolution—from the early web era through cloud computing, big data, machine learning, and now generative AI. As a serial entrepreneur in the 2000s, he co-founded software companies serving clients from startups to local news stations. He later held senior engineering roles at companies from mid-size startups to Fortune 500 enterprises, building video platforms, recommendation engines, and autonomous AI agents.

He holds a Master's degree in Computer Science with a specialization in AI/ML from Western Governors University, completed in 2025 at age 48 while working full-time. He has filed several provisional patents on AI systems and published research on declarative agent orchestration.

Originally from Barcelona, Spain, Ivan has worked across the United States before settling in Silicon Valley in 2015. He lives in Los Gatos, California, with his family.

Connect with Ivan:
LinkedIn: linkedin.com/in/ivan-daunis
Email: idaunis@gmail.com

www.ingramcontent.com/pod-product-compliance
Lightning Source LLC
Chambersburg PA
CBHW071147130626
46553CB00004B/1563